POUNDING THE
ROCK

Basketball Dreams and Real Life
in a Bronx High School

MARC SKELTON

YELLOW JERSEY PRESS
LONDON

1 3 5 7 9 10 8 6 4 2

Yellow Jersey Press, an imprint of Vintage
20 Vauxhall Bridge Road
London SW1V 2SA

Yellow Jersey Press is part of the Penguin Random House group of companies
whose addresses can be found at global.penguinrandomhouse.com.

Penguin
Random House
UK

First published by Yellow Jersey Press in 2019

www.vintage-books.co.uk

A CIP catalogue record for this book is available from the British Library

ISBN 9781787290051

Printed and bound in Great Britain by Clays Ltd, Elcograf S.p.A.

Penguin Random House is committed to a sustainable future for our business,
our readers and our planet. This book is made from Forest Stewardship Council®
certified paper.

To Jessica

When nothing seems to help, I go and look at a stonecutter hammering away at his rock, perhaps a hundred times without as much as a crack showing in it. Yet at the hundred and first blow it will split in two, and I know it was not that last blow that did it, but all that had gone before.

—Jacob Riis

CONTENTS

2016–2017
FANNIE LOU HAMER FREEDOM HIGH SCHOOL BASKETBALL TEAM

TEAM NAME: Panthers

COLORS: Red, White, and Black

SCHOOL ADDRESS: 1021 Jennings Street,
the Bronx, New York 10460

HEAD COACH: Marc Skelton

ASSISTANT COACH: Gaby Acuria, Kyheem Taylor

MANAGERS: Dalen Ward, Mohammed Fofana,
Henry Gonzalez, Alams Beato

NAME	POSITION	HEIGHT	YEAR
Jaelen "JB" Bennett	Guard	5'10"	9
Shamar Carpenter	Shooting Guard	5'9"	12
Kenneth Castro	Shooting Guard	5'7"	11
Charles Davis	Power Forward	6'2"	11
Josh Emanuel	Scorekeeper/Guard	5'10"	10
Bryant Gillard	Center	6'2"	11
Jaquan Mack	Point Guard	5'9"	11
Tyree Morris	Shooting Guard	6'0"	10
Walfri Restitullo	Power Forward	6'2"	12
Cris "Cookies" Reyes	Shooting Guard	5'10"	10
Kaleb Stobbs	Point Guard	5'0"	9
Frankie Williams	Point Guard	5'9"	10

PREFACE

In 2013, the Fannie Lou Hamer Panthers won the New York City Public Schools Athletic League Class B basketball championship. It was the first championship in any sport in school history. What does a coach do after his team has won a championship? He starts writing a book, of course.

For a long while I had wanted to write about basketball. So in the summer of 2013, I started writing about the game I love. Writing was my off-season. It was not something I could do during the school year; teaching responsibilities, coaching obligations, and family duties leave very little time to breathe, never mind write. But during the summer, the noise that's stuck in my head after teaching or coaching is absent.

I didn't know where to send my work. On a whim I sent an email to Ray Anczelowicz, who runs a basketball website called *Gotham Hoops*. We started with a Coaches' Corner piece. Every two weeks or so I would write something about my team, basketball camp, the off-season, the mid-range jump shot, or the NBA playoffs. I developed longer pieces, like "Remember the Yugoslavs: The Death of Yugoslavian Basketball." Even less interesting was "The Banality of Basketball." They were tongue-in-cheek sports ballads with a historical and literary tilt. I enjoyed writing them. It was fun and harmless.

Then one day in August 2014, I got a call from Nancy Mann, at the time the principal at Fannie Lou Hamer Freedom High School. She said a reporter from the *New York Times* had called and wanted to talk to me about basketball.

I had had one strange brush with what we might call "big media" before this. There was a phone call I had in 2006 with someone whose name I have long forgotten. We can just call him Hollywood. He'd somehow learned I was to become the new basketball coach.

"It will look like this. Magic or Bill Bradley will come in and help you coach. We have Magic Johnson on board, and he can move mountains," said Hollywood for an opener.

"You guys were the worst team in New York City last year, right? The school is in a tough area of the Bronx. I've read it is in the poorest urban congressional district in the United States."

Hollywood had done his homework. In the 2005–06 season, the Fannie Lou basketball team was 0-18. The school is located in one of the poorest sections of the country.

"Yeah, but I wasn't even the coach last year."

My attempt to stonewall or build an alibi didn't work. I was a rookie coach, and he knew that.

"That doesn't matter," Hollywood said. "Magic can move mountains."

This was a real phone conversation. I was about to start my first year coaching, and someone already planned to do a reality television show about me and my team. He wanted cameras to follow me and the players around. All I could envision was cheap, badly done television. Another ghetto exploitation film about rough times, drugs, guns, hope, and basketball. As you can probably guess, the Fannie Lou basketball reality television show never happened. As a rule, teachers hate movies about teaching. They seem to always ring false. We witness humanity; we try to prevent failure, we observe children's complete and incomplete metamorphoses, we vouch for their honesty, we mend, we yell, we hush, we give high fives, we give stickers, we watch meltdowns, we clean up *everything*. Anytime anything is

written about schools, I always see the thin line between foster-
ing and exploiting. This phone call was clearly about the latter.

So I wasn't quick to call the *Times* back. I was nervous. Then
I did.

Michael Powell, the *Times* journalist, explained to me that
he had just moved over to the sports section and he'd Googled
something like "The Death of New York City Basketball." I
had written a hackneyed piece on that subject, and Powell
found it. I gave him a witches' brew of reasons why New York
City, while still firmly a basketball city, was not producing NBA
All-Stars at the rate that it once did. I offered up criticisms of
everyone: among them, Amateur Athletic Union (AAU) culture
in general and the Knicks in particular for producing such a bad
product year after year. It was as if a dark cloud, like the one
in *Ghostbusters,* had descended upon the city, causing our hoop
dreams to become haunted ghouls with broken jump shots. Near
the conclusion of our conversation, I invited Powell to tryouts
in October. The next thing I knew, I had two Pulitzer Prize–
winning journalists, Powell and the *Times* staff photographer
Todd Heisler, sitting in the school cafeteria a few minutes before
the start of the 2014–15 season. They were embedded with us all
season. In July 2015 the *New York Times* published a piece titled
"A Long Hardwood Journey" documenting our season.

It was a difficult season for the Fannie Lou Panthers. We were
in a transition year. It felt like we had nine power forwards on
the team. We had a shipload of distractions. Our record was
15 wins, 11 losses.

Did the reporter and the photographer distract us at all
from playing our best basketball? It's hard to say. In retrospect
they probably saved our season. It was as if we had guests over
and needed to be on our best behavior. But unlike guests who
can wear out their welcome quickly, we really enjoyed having

Michael and Todd around simply to talk to. When asked what it was like to pursue the city championship, I said our job was to "harpoon the whale." "Harpooning" has many meanings, as does "the whale." Winning can be the key to unlocking some of life's doors.

The story this book tells is not about one of the greatest teams in New York City basketball history. It is a book that tackles ideas of education in the twenty-first century, self-actualization, brotherhood, failure, courage, and faith. I think it is important to view basketball as a great symbol of enlightenment among uncertainty. I offer you a first-person account, a coach's viewpoint, of the overachieving basketball team at Fannie Lou Hamer Freedom High School as we attempt to win a 2016–17 city championship against the odds. This story is as much about basketball as *Moby-Dick* is about the pursuit of a white whale. Which is to say that something larger than basketball is at stake. This is a portrait of a small school in a big city and of a neighborhood and borough that is continually changing and evolving. But the fact is, they are all winning.

POUNDING THE
ROCK

WARM-UP

It was one of the most important film sessions of the season, and I wrapped it up early. I didn't want us to be late. It was February, and another regular season was coming to an end. A win on Friday most likely would give us home-court advantage for the first two rounds in the citywide playoffs. Lose and we could theoretically play on the road somewhere in Chinatown or the Rockaways, I imagined.

Four o'clock came around, and the team and I grabbed some seats in a classroom. I overheard some complaints on our way up the staircase. There were thoughts and questions, some said out loud, others in a whisper: *What are we doing? We have a game tomorrow, Coach. This is a teachers' meeting, we don't belong here. We're supposed to get ready for the Archimedes game.* Or something along these lines.

Walfri Restitullo, the senior power forward, entered the room and sat down quietly. With his maroon hoodie zipped up and his chin-strap beard a little overgrown, he looked the part of the elder statesman. He had enjoyed a solid senior season, averaging 10 points and almost 9 rebounds a game. As the leader of the team he sat quietly, expecting the others to follow his example. They did.

The previous Tuesday evening we had scored 115 points, a school record, in a win. It was our twenty-second victory of the year. A win on Friday and we would equal the previous year's win total of twenty-three, another school record. This would be an outstanding accomplishment, but we were still haunted by our five-point loss in the 2016 Public Schools Athletic League semifinal game to enjoy it. The accomplishment was somehow sullied by the loss to Jane Addams High School that year. We were anxious for the regular season to finish and for the playoffs to start. But first I wanted the team to attend this teachers' meeting.

Mr. Bob Moses entered the room. We, the students and teachers, were seated, or I should say scattered, across the room. Some of us were standing or leaning against the wall. Some were seated alone at a table while the rest were piled up next to each other like defunct bumper cars. Mr. Moses wore a heather-gray pullover, and a blue-collared shirt poked out around his neck. He had on dark pants and black shoes. He was bald on top, with snow-white hair above his ears and what could be the start of a beard on his face.

Kate Belin, the venerated math teacher at Fannie Lou Hamer Freedom High School, introduced Mr. Moses. I knew I was in the presence of greatness when with a flick of the wrist Mr. Moses asked if we could arrange the tables so we could all be seated. Quickly, the tables were shoved together to form a shape I have seen only in a game of Tetris: a square in the middle with an L-shaped desk married to another irregular S-shaped tetromino. Mr. Moses was silent as tables, chairs, and people were moved into a more intimate setting.

"So, this school is named Fannie Lou Hamer Freedom High School," Mr. Moses began once we were all seated around him. A long pause followed. Then a question. "What's it about?" Mr. Moses had us, the teachers, in rapture, while the team looked nervous. He commanded the room with a whisper.

"I knew Mrs. Fannie Lou Hamer." Once he said this, I knew I should have given the boys a quick primer on Bob Moses, but I wanted to surprise them. He had been the leader of the Student Nonviolent Coordinating Committee, also known by its acronym SNCC. He was instrumental in leading the voter registration drive in Mississippi in 1964, also known as Freedom Summer. I also knew that nobody was worried about our film session anymore. At one of the most important moments of the season, it takes a man of Bob Moses's significance for basketball to drift away from our minds. The guys were locked in.

"Does anyone know when slavery was outlawed in the United States?" Mr. Moses asked mildly. A few eyes shift to me, the history teacher. Of course I am thinking, *1865, Thirteenth Amendment.* Is this a test? I wonder. Before anyone can say anything, he pops another question: "What happened on December seventh, 1941?" Charles Davis, a junior power forward, our leading scorer and rebounder, raises his hand. "Pearl Harbor." Teachers and his teammates nodded proudly.

This was not going to be one of those meetings where you could answer one question and stop paying attention. The gravity of our guest was so powerful that nobody wanted to continue film or even go to the gym. So compelling was Mr. Moses in the first few minutes that Walfri and Charles started taking notes, and soon so did the whole team. Mr. Moses encouraged everyone, including teachers, to take notes. Class was in session.

"Slavery ended with Circular 3591."

"What's that?" everyone in the room was asking themselves.

"Who is the president in 1941?"

Kenneth Castro, a shy junior shooting guard, raises his hand. "Roosevelt."

"Right," Mr. Moses says. "In 1941, December twelfth, Franklin Roosevelt is president. Francis Biddle is the attorney general. He issues Circular 3591 to every state attorney general and tells them from henceforth the FBI is not to prosecute peonage as indebtedness, right? It's to prosecute peonage as indentured servitude and slavery. He's telling these state attorney generals that they have got to stop rounding up young black men for vagrancy, charging them with indebtedness, and sending them off to the slave labor camps to build the steel industry in this country, right?"

Following the Civil War, there was a need for labor on plantations. Local governments discovered a new way to enslave the newly freed slaves of the South. If a man owed money, he could be sent to prison to pay off his debt. Or he could be sent to a nearby plantation and work off his fine. It didn't take long for debt slavery to become institutionalized after the Civil War.

Mr. Moses paused, then continued. "Now, why is Biddle sending out that letter? Because the country has just been attacked. Pearl Harbor, December seventh. And Roosevelt knows he's going to need black soldiers. Slavery officially ended in 1941."

We are a country that "lurches," he said. He explained that in 1787 the United States Constitution was written; then the Civil War of 1861–65, or what he referred to as "the War of Constitutional People over Constitutional Property," was fought; and then another shift in the country happened during what we know as the Reconstruction Era, which Mr. Moses properly called "Redemption." The third era of reform would be the civil rights era, and we are now two-thirds of the way through that. (Although I was thinking that with Donald Trump in the White House, we are not lurching anymore. It looks like we have fallen flat on our faces.)

Voter registration was one of the SNCC's main goals in the 1960s. One of the unforeseen benefits of the vote is being able to take part in another essential part of democracy: selection for jury duty. All-white male juries dominated this country for a long time. When you register to vote, you give yourself another chance to play a role in the judicial system by becoming a juror.

In the twenty-first century, Mr. Moses has focused his lens on algebra as the key to unlocking inequality. Numeracy is one of the deciding factors that determine what kind of career someone can have. But it can also prevent children from graduating college, and even high school. Mr. Moses said, "Algebra is gate-keeper." If you want to participate in a modern economy and go to college, you should have the choice of studying whatever a university offers you. Math is the sentinel that prevents children from studying economics, physics, or engineering. Just as SNCC was a political tool to help black Americans gain political access, he views algebra as the instrument to help fix economic and education inequalities, especially for poor minority students. Now he runs the Algebra Project, of which Fannie Lou has been a member for a long time.

Mr. Moses's questions were heartfelt. His words were edifying. His work was inspiring. He was forming bridges to connect the school's namesake, the civil rights movement, the current political mess, and mathematics.

Mr. Moses spoke of incarceration rates. "Why are there so many men of color in prisons? Why were freed black men arrested after the Civil War?" The answer he offered was that black men could be arrested or fined for almost anything. After the abolition of slavery, southern states started using chain gangs to fill the void left by families migrating north to work the fields. Unable to pay their debts, they soon went to prison. There they worked as if they were slaves in subhuman conditions. Prisons would lease prisoners to farms and plantations.

About thirty minutes into the conversation, Frankie Williams, the sophomore starting point guard, raises his hand. "You know, we are the basketball team." Mr. Moses may have interpreted this statement to mean, "Hey, we are just a bunch of kids, what can we do?" Mr. Moses didn't blink.

"Good. What are you going to do about your school? Your community?"

Mr. Moses had long ago perfected brinkmanship with large crowds. He had us thinking about the country. He had us thinking about history. He had us thinking about the future.

Shamar Carpenter, a senior, and Tyree Morris, a sophomore, were our best three-point shooters. They quietly agreed that something needed to be done. This is how we played. Charles and Walfri, our best rebounders, would catch the fish, and Tyree and Shamar, the ultrafast guards, would fry it.

"I think we have to take care of ourselves, first and foremost," Frankie said.

Frankie, on the other hand, has a pull-yourself-up-by-your-bootstraps attitude that directly conflicts with Mr. Moses's call for us to act for the community collectively. Frankie wants to improve himself, and then he will help others; he sees it as quite dangerous and maybe even a little naive to think you could change someone. Frankie has a conservative streak in him that reminds me of another Bronxite, Colin Powell. Frankie's love for himself was not selfish; it was for his own preservation. This is how kids like Frankie succeed. They take care of themselves, get good grades, stay away from the gangs and drugs, go to college, and find careers.

I don't find Frankie's unwillingness to help out at all strange, because in general Americans work hard, but we don't work hard *collectively*. Mr. Moses was challenging us to ask tough questions about that. How can we work together in a school? In a community? In the classroom and on the court?

I stepped out of the room, leaving the team with Mr. Moses and a few other teachers. These are the moments when I love to coach. I love it when I am surrounded by my basketball team and basketball has faded into the ether. Mr. Moses was convinced algebra would open doors for children. I'm convinced basketball forces them to sit and pay attention in their algebra and physics classes. They work hard in their history and litera-ture classes so they can play. I felt we were doing similar work: providing children with a quality public education. That night in February, with the playoffs knocking on the door, we were talking about something meaningful, not out-of-bounds plays, not shot selection, and not Friday's game. The team was engaged with a man who knows firsthand the dark history of this country, a country where men have been murdered and women beaten and families destroyed and jobs lost simply because they wanted to register to vote and be first-class citizens.

We would win on Friday night. Later, when I asked Walfri what he thought about Mr. Moses, he said, "The first thing that popped up in my mind was that he is quite fit for eighty-two years old." It wasn't the answer I was expecting. Walfri had just met one of the titans of the civil rights movement, a MacArthur Genius Grant winner, and he was most impressed with his fitness. Still, it made sense to me. That's the blessing of life: to be active and interacting with people, trying to fix wrongs, even in the winter of one's life.

PART ONE

THE PRESEASON

WALFRI

Walfri Restitullo has a white towel around his neck and securely tucked into his red practice jersey, and he's bent over, madly pounding the rock against the wood floor. The towel is wet. He's in his fourth year of high school and he's working toward his first championship in his final season. Two years ago, if you had asked me what the likelihood was of Walfri being a starter or the captain, I'm not sure I would have said anything. He had a lot of work to do. And he has done that work, the necessary work, to become a very good player. He was cut his freshman year. His sophomore year he played in only a handful of games. His junior year he displayed a brief but dominating excellence that faded right before the playoffs. All these ups and downs seemed to drive him to show everyone that he was a very good basketball player and he was determined to play consistently. He was the player who learned more in a loss than a victory. He was at times outwardly resistant. But inwardly he was disciplined and self-critical. He was always searching for ways to improve himself. As a six-foot-two-inch power forward, Walfri used his intelligence to gather rebounds. He wasn't able to inhale rebounds off the rim like Charles. Instead he was physical. He wore guys down. He loved to play chess, and he played basketball with a grand-master's mind. There's no doubt in my mind that when Walfri is in his forties, he will be the best player in the Over 40 League. He has a toolbox full of gambits and post moves.

When I think about Walfri's improvement, he may be like no other player I have ever coached. He is now working on his post moves. Up and under. Baby hook. Reverse layup. Now he was averaging close to double digits in points and rebounds. The towel now resembles a yoke.

At this point Walfri looks like a character in Ilya Repin's painting *Barge Haulers on the Volga*. Walfri starts at the baseline dribbling two basketballs. Charles is behind him, holding on to Walfri's hips for added resistance. Charles gets dragged as if he's in an invisible sled past the free-throw line all the way to half-court. They switch roles. Now Charles has to dribble two balls simultaneously while Walfri crouches down and pretends to be an anchor.

At seventeen, sometime next season Charles will leave Fannie Lou as the all-time leader in points, rebounds, blocks, and games played. He's known for his dunks and quiet demeanor. If you were going to go to the beach, you would want to invite Charles. He would carry the coolers, the pails and shovels, inflatable rafts, chaise longues if necessary. Without a doubt, he is the foundation of our defense and offense. Now he is getting a lesson about hard work from Walfri. It seems Walfri carries the success of the team on his back like the towel around his neck. He is his own biggest critic. He works like this all season.

Fatigue has set in. They do this at least a dozen times. Their toil in this gym is laudable. They enjoy the hard work. After the practice was over, Walfri said, "We have a lot of work to do." Only then did I know he could lead us to a championship. He somehow knew that even after a grueling two-hour practice, there was more work to be done. He was like Mr. Bob Moses in that sense. Just because you had gone down to Mississippi and forced the Democrats to include the Mississippi Freedom Democratic Party in the convention as delegates, the work was not done.

Walfri was impeccably cool. Sometimes too cool for school. More than once he had been seen playing cards or dice in school. He retained some habits he had picked up from his block. "I don't see anything wrong with it," he would always declare. "I finished my work."

He was right. He always finished his work. He had an above-90 average. Walfri would stop by my room when he felt stressed-out by another teacher. One time he clearly wanted to see if he could tell me his side of the story before an email or phone call could be made. He'd rushed into my room and said, "Coach, you wouldn't believe what happened." It was always something minor. He cajoled his teachers or used his phone in class. Never anything sordid, but his responses were defensive, not offensive.

Usually it was a case of Walfri wanting to see what boundaries he could push. He felt like he was always respectful until someone disrespected him. Then a verbal confrontation might happen. He was a gentleman until he was pushed, poked, and prodded into something he didn't want to do, like fight. Yet he liked to argue. He was competitive. He wanted to know what you were thinking.

His first two years on the team were about Walfri pushing boundaries with me. Once, when he was a sophomore, he kept asking me why he didn't play. I explained to him he practiced slow, so games would be like if he was on a tricycle at the Indy 500. While he had a smooth jumper, it took him some time to release it, and I said it would be something we could work on in the off-season. He didn't buy it. Therefore he continued to sit on the bench during games.

In the second quarter of a close game during his sophomore year, he went into a game.

We were on the road and it was a lively crowd. On the first possession, Walfri caught the ball near half-court and, before he could turn around, was jumped by two defenders who ripped the ball from him and scored a layup. We made eye contact after the play. He knew I was right. After that moment, Walfri and I had a better understanding of each other. He needed to trust me, and I also needed him to play through mistakes.

"I took strides every day to get better—I practiced any chance I could, morning, noon, and night," Walfri once told me his senior year. I believed him. He became an essential part of the team. I didn't intentionally minimize his playing time his sophomore year to maximize his desire to improve and reap the benefits of his heady play his senior year, but it did seem to work out that way.

He lives with his older brother, younger sister, and mother. His mom is from the Dominican Republic. I never asked about his dad, and Walfri never told me anything about him. He never revealed much of his hardscrabble life in the Hunts Point section of the Bronx. He did share an essay with me that he had written. In it were the things he wanted me to know: how much his mom valued education, how much basketball gave him discipline and a drive to improve himself. But it was the first line that stuck me like a pin. "Have you ever had negative influences everywhere you go?" The second line was even more illuminating. "Or having to be worried that there are dangerous people almost everywhere you go?" I was moved by the absolutes in his questions. Everywhere? In the second line he qualifies it with the adverb "almost," and I would like to think that school, home, and basketball are where he can feel safe.

"You see and hear things you aren't supposed to at a young age," Walfri declared in a text once. The Bronx makes you grow up faster. Fifteen-year-olds mask their real age. Seventeen-year-olds act and function better than most adults I know; they have jobs, cars, some even have children. By nineteen some are ready to retire, having lived a tumultuous life. When you regularly hear about twenty-one-year-olds being murdered, you cannot take your teenage life for granted. Why should it surprise me that when Walfri sees an eighty-two-year-old Bob Moses, he is most impressed that he's eighty-two? He has seen too many young lives cut short.

Walfri plays through pain. His knees hurt after practice, but he never complains. During his junior year he caught an elbow at practice that left a large gash near his left eyebrow. He wears a scar there now. He wore a facemask to practice the next day. In the three years he played for me, he didn't miss one practice. He played sick. He played when things weren't going right at home. He showed the younger kids what it meant to be dedicated. Basketball is where Walfri went to escape the streets and to avoid trouble. The team all followed his lead and worked hard in practice because of him. Every championship team needs a leader like Walfri.

LET'S GO!

Walfri talked a lot about going away to college, about getting out of the Bronx. Without basketball he would need something else to protect him from the streets. College would give him a chance not to stick around the block. As a kid I remember thinking about traveling too. My boyhood dreams were always Melvillean. I wanted a voyage like Darwin, Ulysses, Gagarin, and Melville. I always wanted to be a cosmonaut when I grew up. Since Yuri Gagarin launched into space on April 12, 1961, and my birthday is April 13, 1974, I always thought there was some cosmic connection between us. Right before Yuri was launched into space, he said "Poyekhali," meaning "Let's go" in Russian. Interestingly, while Boston remains my birthplace, it is Derry, New Hampshire, that I have to call my adoptive home. Derry is the birthplace of Alan Shepard, the first American in space.

When we moved there, I thought it was another sign that I was going to go to space. My mother said I was always talking about it. The idea almost got me killed once.

Dressed in a snowsuit two sizes too big, I sat unbridled in the front seat of my family's 1975 Dodge Charger, aching with the boredom only a five-year-old knows. My eyes were fixed on the blood-orange flame of the radio, glowing like a fireplace. The danger mesmerized me, even though I knew I would be burned if I touched it. Then the glove compartment stole my attention for a few moments. I turned the bulky silver knob. Open. Close. Open. Close.

Taking her eyes off the road and peering down at me, my mother warned, "Leave that alone, we are almost home."

My attention turned back to the nuclear glow from the radio. My mother had strict rules about touching the radio. When she drove the car, she steered the dials of the FM too. I knew if I touched it, I would get slapped.

I rested my head on the console and let my mind drift like the floating thighbone in Kubrick's *2001: A Space Odyssey*. I pushed the door with my feet. The instrument panel was broken. My mother never knew how fast we were going or how much fuel we had or whether the door was fully closed. I kept pushing the door, although I believed it was locked. What would happen if the door opened? The idea grew in my mind like space. How far would I fly if I opened the door? I sat upright and timed my premature departure. I grabbed the metallic handle, took a deep breath, and pulled. *Poyekhali!* Immediately I was ejected into space. It is difficult to say how far I traveled; my eyes were closed. When I opened them I was either in orbit or in a snowbank. It was the first time I remember being alone and excited. I escaped and I survived. I was proud of my feeble attempt to be an asteroid or meteor, whichever one rockets across the sky. I can never remember which one is which.

My mother's voice pierced the snow mound. *Sound can't travel in space.* I was still on earth.

"Marc! Marc!" my mom was screaming, louder than the time I hid in the clothes rack at Kmart. Her hot, panicked voice was coming closer, and I could feel other people, like satellites, surrounding me.

My frozen voice couldn't escape my mouth, never mind the snow cave. I lay silently, listening to the panic in my mother's voice grow stronger. The snow had swallowed me up. I was shoeless too. I was trapped in the belly of a whale, like Jonah, with wet socks. The red lights turned the billions of snow crystals the color of blood. But I'm cool staying where I am because I know when she finds me I will be banished to the backseat. There were more people and more lights. *Sound doesn't travel in space.*

My mother found my moon boots, and my first thought was I should have changed the radio station instead.

"What the hell were you thinking?"

She whacked me on top of my head with the heel of the snow boot. The snowsuit wouldn't let my arms above my shoulders.

"Are you all right?" I heard.

Another gravity-induced smack was applied to the exact same spot. I raised my arms to protect my head, but the snowsuit limited my range of motion.

The interrogation continued, and it was brutal. I couldn't even answer the questions before I was leveled. My mom was roughing me up more than jumping out of a moving car did. She continued to hit me in the black night with my snow boot, canceling my career as a cosmonaut. My feet were getting cold. One of the Good Samaritans who'd gathered suggested she take me to the hospital to see if I'd broken anything in the fall. Blind old bat, couldn't she see I had my snowsuit on?

"He's fine."

I was fine.

Mom swatted my head again. "Get in the car," she said.

I knew fireflies didn't fly in the winter. Yet they are everywhere. The stars in orbit made me even dizzier. That was the first time I tried to escape. I owe my life to the person who invented snowsuits.

As the years passed, I came to regard my cosmic slumber in the ice pod as a haven, however brief it was. Whenever I felt comfortable, I also had this uneasy feeling it wouldn't last. And anytime I found solace, my mom would arrive and rip it from me. I dreamed about having more than she could take away, and I played hoops more to be alone, to create a gap that separated me from her and my stepdad, until their transgressions receded from my mind. Nothing made sense without basketball.

She told my stepfather what I did when we got home. He mumbled something and continued watching television. He was an alien to me. I never really knew him. Always quiet, foreboding, never really interested in anything, not mountaineering, not race cars, only his mashed potatoes and gravy that he'd wash down with vodka mixed with orange juice.

On April 12, 2009, forty-eight years after Yuri Gagarin launched into space for the first time, my first daughter Nina was born. Later on I discovered Yuri loved basketball. He said it helped him get through astronaut school. He also became a basketball coach. There are some strange cosmic connections that we can't really explain in life.

SCHOOL AND SCHOOLMASTERS

On October 5, 1977, President Jimmy Carter toured the Bronx and called Charlotte Street and the surrounding area the worst slum in America. When you look at photos from the seventies, it appears as if an asteroid smashed into the Bronx, causing the kind of damage that only something from outer space could have. I have never seen photos that make me think of silence more. If sound doesn't travel in space, these photographs convey the silence of a kind of social outer space. Three years later, Ronald Reagan returned and claimed Carter hadn't fixed a thing.

A few blocks from Charlotte Street is a two-toned ginger-bread brick building located at the corner of West Farms Road and Jennings Street in the Bronx. The building was once a nondescript factory, indistinguishable amid the archipelago of former factories in the Bronx.

The school was once a garment factory for those recovering from tuberculosis or depression; I like to think of it as a sanitarium for the convalescing who needed a job. Now it's a high school for anyone in the neighborhood who wants a sound education.

Little is known about the Altro Health and Rehabilitation Services Workshop, except that on March 13, 1958, Nom Lee, a Chinese immigrant and employee, shot and killed a coworker and held the other two hundred employees hostage. I have packaged this grisly fact into a ghost story retold with great gusto to unexpecting eleventh graders every Halloween.

What else is known about the Altro factory is that its name was a shortened version of "altruistic," an attempt to help people who may not have been able to work elsewhere. The workshop was founded in 1913 by Jewish philanthropies. Over a century later, altruism still echoes within the walls at 1021 Jennings Street. Fannie Lou Hamer Freedom High School has become one of the best beat-the-odds schools in the world.

What odds? The odds of a child in a middle-class family in the 1980s earning more than her parents in her lifetime was less than 50 percent. Social mobility has been unplugged. For a few decades we kept putting bread into the toaster, waiting for the toaster to turn on. Then we start yelling at the bread, "What's wrong with you?" We shake the toaster and give it a whack. Finally, we give up, throw away the toaster, and find something else to eat. So what do you think the odds are of someone born into poverty in this century making it out of poverty?

Social mobility has plateaued in the United States; in fact, the race-wealth gap has quadrupled in the last thirty years. The climb up the shaky economic ladder has always been, to say the least, an obstacle-filled journey. Eighteen years into the new millennium, and more and more Americans are born without rungs on their ladders. In America, there is a certain pathos we feel for those who climb out of poverty, and a certain disappointment we harbor for those who don't.

Anchored in the poorest urban congressional district in the United States and one of the most segregated sections in New York City, Fannie Lou has been the touchstone for small school success in the city for more than twenty years. Fannie Lou may not be the holy grail of high schools, but it is damn close. Emma Lazarus would have written a poem about this school. Imagine a school where everyone is welcomed. Too old? Come on in. Didn't get the right score on the state exam? No problem. You were absent a lot of days in middle school? You had to take care of your mother? You had to translate for her too? You have a kid? How old are you? It doesn't matter, have a seat. *Bienvenidos a Estados Unidos! Si, aquí tu hijo puede entrar la escuela. Si, gratis.* You can't pass the Regents Exams? Don't worry, we got you. Your high school closed? How many? Twenty students? Sure, come on in.

How does a school educate those who don't have decent housing, who don't have the proper eyeglasses, who don't have books on their nightstands, food in the refrigerator, extra cash around the house to pay for incidentals, a quiet place to do homework? Let me say it is not easy.

Fannie Lou Hamer Freedom High School was designed to welcome all students; more specifically, to offer kids in the Bronx a sound high school education. It attempts to widen the narrow opportunities available in the Bronx. Our college guidance counselors were able to help the class of 2017 receive more than $1.5 million in college scholarships.

In the last twelve years in New York, small schools with a student population of five hundred students have increasingly replaced the large comprehensive high schools, those with over two thousand students, throughout the city. More and more small high schools have been created this century. As a result, high school graduation rates in New York City have also improved steadily over the last ten years. The credit has been given to Mayor Michael Bloomberg, but the teachers, staff, administrators, students, and their families also deserve some as well.

Fannie Lou was one of the first small high schools in New York City. It was created in 1993 when the Board of Education and the State Education Department closed James Monroe High School in the Bronx. After many years of ineptitude and neglect, six small high schools were born to correct the abysmal, if not criminal, 26.9 percent graduation rate of James Monroe High School in 1992. Without reservation I can say Fannie Lou is the beacon of the small schools movement. Smaller high schools with smaller student bodies, particularly those that serve the communities of its surrounding neighborhoods, can operate like a village, where students, teachers, and parents get to know and support each other better. This proximity fosters stronger, more intimate relationships and increases student engagement.

To see why Fannie Lou was chosen by the National Education Policy Center as a Gold Medal School of Opportunity, simply look at our graduation rate. In 2017, Fannie Lou's graduation rate was 68 percent. A 40 percent increase in the graduation rate while serving children from the same neighborhood speaks volumes about the work Fannie Lou Hamer Freedom High School has accomplished.

What makes Fannie Lou such an incredible place? First, imagine an environment where students and teachers can treat school as an intellectual community. Second, teachers don't just hand out worksheets and wait for the bell to ring. Students are asked to be active learners, not passive participants. They study the Bronx River not only by visiting it, but by building boats and rowing the only freshwater river in New York City. They learn math by building dodecahedrons out of plywood. They participate in internships across the city. Fannie Lou prepares students to live productive lives after high school.

TRYOUTS: OCTOBER 5, 2016

I was concentrating like a blackjack dealer, shuffling through creased parental consent documents, juggling physical forms, searching for the parent's signature, hunting for physicians' registry numbers, vigilant that no one was trying to cheat and sneak into tryouts. Kyheem Taylor, Luis Padilla, and Gaby Acuria, the assistant coaches, were playing gatekeepers: denying entry to anyone without the proper paperwork, counting the number of boys in the gym, drawing invisible lines from names to faces the way skilled teachers memorize new students on the first day of school. I thought I needed to see my doctor soon too. Rarely did I question my fitness as a coach, a teacher, a father, or a husband, but at that moment I did. I'm not convinced coaching basketball is the healthiest thing I could be doing. A few seasons ago, a fellow PSAL coach died from a brain aneurysm at forty-four years old. Former Wake Forest coach Skip Prosser died from a heart attack at fifty-six. It is easy to lose yourself in this game. This season I promised myself to exercise more, go to yoga, and eat better.

"All set. Twenty-seven. Let's go. Circle up."

The gym was warm with excitement. Twenty-seven young men tried to squeeze around the red circle at half-court.

"Welcome to Fannie Lou basketball," I announced. "We are looking for a few guys who are committed to team basketball."

The October after-school sun turned the gym the color of Doritos. Tryouts are the annual tradition of trying to figure out who will taste good in January. A new team reminded me of the empty glass jars we would fill with fruit and vegetables in Moldova, where I taught in the Peace Corps. In the fall the jars sat near the kitchen window full of sunshine. The sedate gold lids wore sweaters of cobwebs before we would fill them with peppers, tomatoes, and cucumbers. I loved canning food and preparing jams in the fall so we could eat fruits and vegetables in the winter. What you need every fall is to select a few salted big men who love to rebound, a sprinkling of dried dedicated defenders, and a plump peach who sets bruising picks, then put them on the shelf, where they will help you get through the long winter months.

"I don't like hero basketball," I continued. "Actually, I hate it. If you think this team needs you, you should probably leave now. We have a wrestling team if you want to compete for individual honor or glory."

Basketball is a simple game. On offense we want to take the highest-percentage shot available: layups, open three-pointers, and foul shots. We avoid the mid-range game, those shots inside the three-point arc and outside the paint. On defense we are going to pressure the ball and create turnovers. Those turnovers result in easy baskets.

It sometimes takes years for players to be able to understand the science, math, and psychology of Fannie Lou basketball. I like to think of our team as the San Antonio Spurs of the PSAL. They found a winning formula by selecting talent from overseas. We have a lot of kids on the team whose parents were born overseas. There's a hunger and a toughness in them that I admire and really like coaching. Walfri shows it every day. Charles cannot be stopped when he's going to grab a rebound. Once Frankie Williams decides to drive to the hoop, it's over.

As a coach, I have exploited these attributes along with teaching and demanding team basketball over hero ball. How can we run an egalitarian offense when children are at their narcissistic peak? We throw away the unhealthy junk food that feeds bad teams: poor shot selection, one-on-one basketball, defensive and offensive irresponsibility. We stress an unyielding pressure on defense, especially on the ball. I know I will never tame the New York City player inside them, nor do I want to. I just want to create a team-first attitude with a no-nonsense approach to the game.

I concluded my harangue by saying, "That championship banner behind you is lonely. The only way that banner gets some company is with a team-first agenda."

The 2013 championship banner nailed to the porcelain plaster did in fact look lonely. The year 2013 might as well have been 1993 on the time horizon of the kids encircling me. They were in middle school the last time we won a championship. I thought about the guys on the 2013 team. They are legends, justifiably so. All we needed this year were a few guys who, like our 2013 squad, had a peculiar propensity to make the extra pass and play defense.

"Okay. We are good." I looked at Frankie.

"Let's stretch," Frankie Williams, our intelligent sophomore point guard, barked. Frankie is cereal-box handsome. His good looks belie his competitive fire. His face belonged at your kitchen table to greet you in the morning. He had a vague resemblance to Trayvon Martin and the singer Usher. I first met Frankie when he was in sixth grade, and he has always had a great attitude and vision about his future, the school, and the team. Frankie came to Fannie Lou because he "felt like there are a lot of opportunities for minorities. If you use school the right way, you'll see the world from a different perspective."

As a freshman he recognized right away that if he knew the plays and played defense, he could get playing time. He became a starter after the third game. I probably should have started him the first game. Our gym is the size of a garden shed. The new and returning kids followed his orders and began warming up. Arms swung like shears, and legs kicked like the handles of shovels and rakes dancing in the air.

I heard the wood creak for the first time this season. Years ago a pipe burst in the middle of the winter, flooding the gym. The wood, as is nature's order, swallowed up the water; the court now has Band-Aid-like replacement panels, is warped in other spots, and in certain sections is like the old deck of a seasoned ship. If you run your hand on it, it feels like a worn bannister, especially at half-court, where the replacement wood meets the antediluvian wood and forms twists and turns.

This is also where we love to trap the ball on defense. This is our version of mayhem: the perfect marriage of chaos and discipline. Imagine how difficult it is to dribble a ball when two ravenous defenders are running at you; it is even more difficult to get out of the trap when the ball feels like Phil Niekro just rubbed sandpaper all over it and it dances away from your fingertips as the defenders close in. There are invisible speed bumps all over the blond wood that slow down the game like a despotic governor strategically creating traffic jams on a holiday weekend. I have to hammer in the nails on the replacement boards each year. Yet there is still a sacred geometry intact on our court. It is not congruent with other high school gyms. The typical high school gym is eighty-four feet in length and fifty feet in width. Never mind what the dimensions are in our gym. All I'm going to say is, our gym is small and opposing teams know it is a pain in the ass to play here.

The black volleyball rectangle is surrounded by a larger concentric red rectangle. There is a dotted red line that perforates the court into halves from rim to rim. A sheepish, somnolent black panther rests at half-court. Saucer-size golden coins hide the pits for the volleyball poles, for now covered like mini-manholes. The industrial low-pressure sodium lights cast a mustard sunset; they create a perpetual twilight effect. The white brick walls were painted in August and still have some luster left. Up above, a few dangling ceiling tiles look like giant frosted Mini Wheats. If the size of the court or the surface doesn't give us advantage enough, there is the school's all-time leader in blocked shots: the obtrusive white heating duct that runs the length of the ceiling and makes three points from the right wing all but impossible.

The team sat encircling Frankie, some reaching for their toes, one or two cupping their new sneakers with their palms. One new kid in an orange Knicks shirt, whose fishbowl belly wouldn't let him touch his toes, sat unnoticed by his peers, defeated before the first bounce of a ball. Everyone had their eyes closed. Frankie yelled out the odd numbers and the chorus barked back the even: "One, two, three, four, five, six, seven, eight, nine, ten!" "Everyone count," someone demanded, as if making the pre-practice count loud would somehow lessen the brutal two-hour tryout. Or was the uniformity of counting together somehow important to the start of the season? This was the first ritual as a new team. There was a certain calmness in the gym as Frankie, looking like the hub of a bicycle wheel, sat encircled, the team creating radii around him. Their legs formed uneven spokes, the colorful neon socks and array of loud sneakers looking like rainbow spoke beads on a child's bike. It was a new season. There was a sense of freshness and innocence, like a baby's first tooth. A new team was being born.

There was a choreographed sequence of stretches: first the hamstrings, then the quads, then the IT band stretch; it felt like a yoga studio, an ashram in the Bronx.

As the team stretched, my stomach was throwing scorching fireballs, disguised as burps, into my throat. Was I nervous? Did I drink too much coffee? I drank some water. The lukewarm water from the fountain only made the burning worse. I leaned against the red padding on the wall. It was ripped and torn and had tiny holes, as if a hungry caterpillar lived in the gym. The walls were a two-tiered system of stacks of porcelain and pumpkin-colored cement blocks. The five windows above let in the hum of the traffic on the Sheridan Expressway. Yet before I could start posting quotes from the Bhagavad Gita, the silence was broken when the gym door was yanked open.

"Yo, Frankie, get outta there. Seniors get the center of the circle!"

Xavier Rivera, along with Walfri and Shamar Carpenter one of three returning seniors, proprietarily sauntered into the gym. He was wearing a blue T-shirt and jeans. Bespectacled, he carried his goggles in a small black case. We'd received donations over the summer, and I was able to purchase sports goggles with corrective lenses for X.

"No, X. You're late and he's right. Get dressed, get warmed up. Let's go," I stabbed back.

My voice cracked with fury. I smashed the tranquillity. As you can see, I'm more of an *Enchiridion* guy than a yogi. X's lateness and arrogance destroyed the Vipassanā meditation vibe, and the devotional *om mani padme hum* sprinted out of the gym. The tension grew, but everyone stayed silent. I don't recommend beginning a season by berating a senior; yet I had been transformed into a modern manticore haunting an underprepared, overconfident upperclassman because of some presumed hierarchy.

Here lies the paradox of coaching: I liked Xavier. He had played since he was a freshman. Recklessly yelling at him was like an act of vandalism. Senior year carried with it a sort of heightened status; it meant you had experience and you'd reached the pinnacle of the high school sports hierarchy. I'd just spray-painted all over Xavier's senior year.

When you coach from the heart, there is also a relentless push for justice, for better access to opportunities, to wear better uniforms and sneakers, to find ways to get eyeglasses for guys who have trouble seeing, or an extra pair of socks, another sweatshirt, for fairness, for equality, for better self-esteem. How can I expect them to perform at their best when we have Yeltsin-era uniforms? New sneakers and uniforms are a tiny shield against the gargantuan hardships of growing up in the Bronx. If I want my guys to live healthy, productive lives later on, the years we spend together need to be transformative.

X's head hung low like a question mark, the weight of the embarrassment crushing him. He slowly got dressed and joined the circle. I could have said, "Namaste, Xavier, can I have your papers please, join us in the circle" or "He's right, Frankie, seniors lead us." But I didn't. How could I be so uncharitable?

Twenty-eight teenage boys hopped, squatted, and swiveled on the worn hardwood; fifty-six sneakers squeaked with delight at the start of the new season. This immense pursuit, which sometimes turns manic, starts with an ambitious image of us holding the championship trophy uncomfortably high over our heads, as we awkwardly grasp a white banner, cameras flash, and we inexplicably are never looking at the right camera at the right time. I am stuck on the pursuit of the feeling when you win. I am stuck on this dream: to hope, to pray, this is the key to winning a championship. I know it doesn't work if the right people aren't leading us. But if the right kids can help us, we can achieve our goal. I believe basketball can add a rung to the socioeconomic ladder. It can be a tailwind for kids who face headwinds every day. Yet I just made things really uncomfortable for a young man I have known since he was thirteen.

Xavier Rivera came into the season as he had the previous three: burdened with expectations. I thought he could be the leader, the savvy veteran who helps the young guys with the ups and downs of the season. Xavier had always worked hard. He was a solid student. He was going to compete with Shamar and Tyree Morris for the shooting guard spot. If he didn't start, he could be an excellent sixth man, a spark off the bench. At least Xavier had his seniority; that is, until I graffitied all over it. The hierarchy doesn't function well if the underclassmen are better, and everyone knows it. It's a fallacy. And of course we still had Xavier penciled in as our starting shooting guard. He had added a lot of muscle in the off-season. He had once scored 53 points in eighth grade. We hoped he could add some of his experience and strength to this relatively young team.

"X, do you have your paperwork?" I now asked calmly.

"Here it is," he said, sounding wounded but respectful at the same time.

The glass ceiling of high school sports can be cruel. Xavier's entrance into the gym reminded me we needed to elect captains. Some years I have the team vote, and other years Gaby, Kyheem, Luis, and I will talk it over and decide. Another, more important election cast a shadow on who would be our leader on and off the court.

With the ashram destroyed, we needed to step outside, not just for some fresh air, but also because the gym was starting to smell worse than a Bikram studio. Someone forgot to put deodorant on. New team. New smells.

We exited the gym to Boone Avenue. For the past two decades, the area around the school has been surrounded by car-repair garages and wholesale tire stores where signs hang that simultaneously want to run diagnostics on your muffler and praise Jesus. A few years ago, construction began to bring mammoth apartment buildings to the neighborhood. For the past two years as I biked along 161st Street and Boston Post Road to work each day, I inspected the progress of the future. Adjacent to Fannie Lou, the power brokers were building a gigantic fifteen-story apartment complex. There was a set of staircases that were perfect for preseason conditioning.

"Grab a partner about the same size as you. Put them on your shoulders and carry them up the stairs," I ordered.

Running up the stairs with another person on your back has nothing to do with basketball. Perhaps only Walfri, the senior forward, understood what I was doing. I wasn't inflicting a new tool of sadistic tyranny; I genuinely believed that running up a staircase with another human on your back, your potential teammate, would mold the team. If they balked, they would never trust me, or I them. I'm in love with the idea of hope. Coaching, teaching, parenting, living: we all struggle, and we all need someone to love us. The game rarely loves us back. In tryouts I was looking for someone who had the strength to carry on, even with another human tied to his back.

The leading candidate for captain was Walfri. He had the best grades and best post moves on the team. He was vertically challenged, but his rebounding skills were all technique. He would use his body to move people in what coaches call a box-out. He was also the best dressed. The guy with the best fashion sense was also our blue-collar, hard-hat, lunch-box guy. He was always the first one at practice and would be the first one in his family to go to college. He had a 100 percent attendance record at practice. Over the past three years, he had emerged as a quiet leader who avoided confrontations. He was the obvious choice to be captain.

After tryouts I felt something was missing. I'll admit, it was strange not to see the cast from last season; gone were Jorge, Tim, Shateek, Jeider, Kobe, and Travis. The three seniors, Walfri, Xavier, and Shamar, were not the best players on the team. We needed to fill new roles, and I was unsure whom to cast. The forecast was murky and uncertain if the younger guys were more talented than the upperclassmen. Could Frankie, only a sophomore and the most talented guard, lead us, along with Walfri, without alienating Shamar and Xavier?

We were too young to win it all this year, I thought, but maybe we could win it next year. We had other roles to fill: Who was going to be the glue guy—the player who leads the team in high fives, in charges taken, and makes winning plays? The defensive stopper—the kid who sacrifices all his energy on the defensive end? We needed a hype man—the guy who was always in a good mood, regardless of playing time or the score. At the end of the bench would be the 30–30 guy—the kid who doesn't play unless we are up 30, down 30, or with 30 seconds to play. Who would that be? I had more questions than answers.

There's no junior varsity or freshman team at Fannie Lou Freedom High School. Of the five hundred students, fewer than two hundred are boys. The twenty-odd boys who were trying out impressed me, but the gym was crowded. The intensity of tryouts can wilt the enthusiasm of a few, while the undeterred become managers, shot-clock operators, statisticians, and camera operators. All are a vital part of the team.

After tryouts I was riding home and I realized that today, October 5, was the thirty-ninth anniversary to the day that President Jimmy Carter visited the Bronx. I rode up Charlotte Street. It was a sunny and windless evening. Not a lot going on at six p.m. in this pocket of middle-class single-family homes. Cars parked in their driveways. A menacing blue jay stood near a pile of leaves waiting to be carried off somewhere. In my mind there's a suburban feel to Charlotte Street in the middle of the Bronx that is unique. It would be picturesque to say nobody was going to get cut, but that was not the case.

The day of the second tryout, we walked over to 174th Street. In the shade it was a little chilly for October. I found a warm spot on the corner of 174th and Bryant Avenue. Part of the preseason package is to run outside when the girls' volleyball team is using the gym. Xavier and Shamar complained of back pain. A couple of new guys tapped out and said their asthma was acting up. Without inhalers or pumps, we made them stop running. Were they simply out of breath, out of shape, asphyxiating, or telling the truth? Always better to be safe. I also knew after a few days of training like this that most kids quit.

"Is this a gym class?" A short, middle-aged Latina with golden hair approached the corner.

Nope. A basketball team.

"I used to live on this block. I went to school at P.S. 66." Her sunglasses reminded me that I never wear mine. "When I was a little girl, we moved here from Puerto Rico. The slumlords used to set that building on fire all the time. Till this day, if I smell smoke I get scared."

These boys should be grateful it is not like this anymore. Wow. This block has really changed. Those houses weren't there. "It was buildings like those," she said, pointing to the five-story walk-ups, "that used to burn."

The guys ran up and down the hill. I moved out of the way, and she snapped a photo of the street signs and disappeared.

Charles, Frankie, and Tyree were in the lead. The returning juniors were next: Jaquan Mack, Bryant Gillard, and Latrell Anderson ran next to Walfri. Just shortly behind them were some newcomers: Cris Reyes, Kenneth Castro, Jaelen Bennett, Bari Higinio, and Kaleb Stobbs.

Later, a large black man in gray sweatpants with an incredibly painful gait stopped us. It looked like there was an invisible horse between his legs. He straddled the sidewalk with his grade-school daughter.

"Your guys sure can run!"

"Thanks. Hope to put some points on the board this year," I said.

"I'm sure you will. Best of luck."

"Thanks," I said.

At the third tryout, there were a few new faces, but I still counted twenty-eight kids. The old moved swiftly and the new awkwardly, their bodies quickly approaching manhood, their minds burdened with the prospect of getting cut, their muscles aflame, and their lungs wheezing as they ran up and down the court. Sweat dripped from their temples like a leaky faucet. They would pause and try to catch their breath. "Keep your hands off your knees. We don't show other teams we are tired," Walfri demanded respectfully. "We want to see other teams grab their knees."

It reminded me of the scene from *Star Wars* when Han Solo warns C-3PO to let the Wookie win or he might lose a limb. I felt like I should have warned the freshmen: *Don't upset the Wookie. Freshmen don't pull people's arms out of their sockets when they lose. Seniors do!*

Walfri was like our Chewbacca. He was the ultimate best friend: loyal, dependable, and bright. The exhausted newcomers stared at him respectfully. The new guys looked like broken parentheses, bent at the hip, eyes pinched, craning their necks to listen. They had just enough time to correct their posture before the next drill started.

"Two versus six," I called out. For ten minutes we look like a rugby team. The objective is to move the ball the length of the court against six defenders placed in pairs every fifteen feet. The offense can only pass in order to move the ball down the court. They are not allowed to dribble. This was everyone's least favorite drill, except for Frankie. When he was on defense, the offensive player would wilt like a flower. When he was on offense, he zipped passes and cut sharply.

I love this drill. It makes us better. It forces guys to cut sharp and correctly. The defense has a huge advantage, and it helps us make fewer turnovers. Frankie clapped his hands.

At that moment I knew Frankie and Walfri should lead this team. Frankie had a fluent and intelligent game. He was a smart, confident young man who had acquired those invisible, indispensable skills that never show up in the box score, but that all winning coaches know when they see them. He wore black mesh shorts and last year's red and white practice jersey. Frankie is a unicorn. While his talent is rare, his attitude may be extinct. This wasn't some bull. He plays without an ego with only one objective: to win. Like most of the returning team, Frankie struggled to score in the playoffs last year. He had shown flashes that he was capable of scoring a lot of points, but I wasn't sure he could sustain it the whole season. It would be a heavy burden to be a captain and a starting point guard as a sophomore, but I believed in Frankie.

COACH C

Tryouts were always difficult. They have to be for several reasons. I'm not making decisions weighed over time. I'm watching to see: Who can fight through cramps? Who is going to help us win? Who can stick it out? (Our whole program is a formula to help improve lives, disguised as intense basketball immersion.)

Where did I learn to coach like this? From Anthony Salvatore Carnovale, or as everyone called him, Coach C, my high school basketball coach. Tryouts were always brutal. In high school I threw up during the first tryout four straight years.

In eighth grade Coach C took me to my first Celtics game. Before my seat belt was buckled, I asked, "Is Larry going to play?"

It was a Tuesday, a school night, in May 1989, and we were driving south on Route 93 to the Boston Garden. The muffler on his Toyota pickup truck rattled louder and louder. Larry Bird had played only six games that season because of heel surgery to remove bone spurs. In my fifteen-year-old mind, he had to play. Bird was the one reliable adult in my life. The Celtics were playing the menacing Detroit Pistons in Game Three of the NBA playoffs. Detroit had knocked the Celtics out of the playoffs the previous season, ending a streak of four straight years the Boston Celtics were in the NBA Finals. I was having a difficult time comprehending how a year ago the Celtics were the number-one seed in the East, but now they were the eighth. Why wasn't Bird playing? His ankle had to be better by now. Detroit had won the first two games easily. And tonight, Game Three, at a time when the first round of the playoffs was the best of five, I expected Larry Bird to do what he had always done: rescue the Celtics against the Bad Boys of Detroit. Two years earlier, Bird had stolen the ball late in Game Five against Detroit, in one of the most incredible plays in basketball history, and I wanted him to do it tonight again.

"Probably not," said Coach Carnovale.

With Bird unable to play, I realized the Pistons had started digging the grave for the Celtics a year ago in 1988. I wasn't going to my first Celtics game—I was going to their funeral. It was over. Danny Ainge had been traded earlier that season, breaking up one of the best starting fives in basketball history.

Nineteen eighty-nine was a pivotal year: I was headed to high school, my favorite basketball team was falling apart, before the year was finished the Berlin Wall would be destroyed, and I would be living with a different family. The winds of change were definitely blowing.

"How's school going? How's your mom doing? How's your brother and sister?" Coach C asked.

Those were the first three questions he would pepper me with every time I saw him. He had called me a few days earlier, asking me if I wanted to go to the game. I don't think he knew that I had never seen the Celtics play. I'm sure he knew I led my Boys Club team to a championship in March. In retrospect, this may have seemed like some sort of recruiting violation; high school coach takes promising eighth-grade prospect to a Celtics playoff game. It wasn't. I had attended Coach C's basketball camp since I was seven. He also knew I played at the Boys Club because I was ineligible to play for my middle school team. Nominally, the Boys Club team competed against other Boys and Girls Clubs around New Hampshire. But it was really a team of flunkies like me, or kids who got cut from the middle school team. I wasn't in school much that year. At one point, I added up my in-school and out-of-school suspension days and it was easily over seventy days. Now there were a few weeks left in eighth grade, and in the fall I would be headed to the high school where this guy coached.

Here was a coach who saw a kid at risk. He also knew what basketball meant to a kid who didn't have a lot. Coach C was born in Italy in 1946, a year after the war, and moved to the United States in 1955. I never realized what that really meant until one day, in my early twenties, I had just sat through a double feature at the Brattle Theatre in Cambridge. Roberto Rossellini's *Rome, Open City* and Vittorio De Sica's *Bicycle Thieves* made me think about Anthony Salvatore Carnovale as a toddler in postwar Italy. I don't think he had a lot either, but he knew the power of sports. He taught us about loyalty and standards. We would joke after three-hour practices that he must have inherited his policy of cruelty from Il Duce. He referred to me as a "prima donna." He was a shrewd tactician. He outworked other coaches. He had a scouting report *on officials*. He knew which refs he could torture and which ones to leave alone. He called Taco Bell "Taco King." He loved the positive side of sports, and the negative side ate him up. He thought the bar should be raised within the coaching profession. He felt like there were some very bad people who were also poor coaches and had too much influence on the game. He was right. I was a prima donna.

"Larry Bird is out indefinitely," he added.

The words hung in the air. The phrase reminded me how in the movies an alien spaceship always hovers close to earth, but never lands. Because it was indefinite, it might land tonight, or tomorrow. It could not mean never again.

Coach C's wave of success was a few years behind the Celtics. His team had won a state championship in 1988 but failed to repeat in the championship game in 1989. My freshman year, 1990, I would be on the bench for his second championship. I didn't play a second, but I was there and that was enough. I was hooked on winning. My own basketball career would be set on one thing and one thing only: winning a state championship. After two years of disappointment, finally, my senior year, we made it back to the University of New Hampshire's Lundholm Gym for the state championship game. The gym, as most gyms are in March, was filled to capacity, with almost three thousand people in attendance. We were expected to win the state championship that year. Four out of the five starters—Gregg Brander, Jeremy Thissell, Michael Catizone, and I—had been playing together on the playground since third grade. We were up three, 14–11, at halftime. We were napalmed in the second half and lost 61–41. The thought of that loss still hurts.

I started following basketball in 1983, the year Bird scored 53 points in a single game, and now in 1993, our careers, mine and Bird's, were done. It was a marvelous decade: the eighties and a couple of years into the nineties were about winning and losing championships, and also a time to think about what happens after basketball. A seed was planted when Boston was swept from the playoffs that May night in 1989, and it grew in tandem with my basketball dreams. What arrived after the state championship loss was reality or life after basketball. The spaceship landed.

The game in March 1993 would be my last. Occasionally I look at photographs of the game. There was a VHS tape floating around years ago, but I don't know where it went. I would never watch the second half anyway. After the game, I remember the West High School coach coming up to me and saying, "You're one tough son-of-a-bitch. I would want you on my team any day." I felt more embarrassed than complimented. My coup de grâce had come against them a year earlier when we lost to West by a bucket. I blessed the opposing fans, team, and coaching staff with a double middle-finger salute. I wanted to tell him off again, but I was too heartbroken. We all were. What we didn't know at the time was that would be Coach Carnovale's last championship game. The game of basketball is a mysterious force, its future as cloudy as a crystal ball in a muddy field. I grew up dribbling on gravel, where the ball behaves unpredictably. I should have known better than to try to harness the game.

The other four starters on the team, Gregg, Jeremy, Michael, and Chris Hunt, would go on to play college basketball. Off the bench, Mike Jean would also go on to play at the next level, graduate from Saint Anselm College with a degree in history, and move to San Diego. Chip Allen would get a degree in graphic design. John Drelick went to Hofstra University with a degree in finance and is now a public accountant. Chris Hunt is now a principal at a middle school in New Hampshire.

Gregg Brander has a degree in mathematics. Jeremy Thissell is a lawyer in Maryland. Some of the other guys I have lost touch with. The majority of us went to college, graduated, and are now entering middle age with children of our own. Over those four years in high school, a few of us on the team didn't have fathers. But most of the guys on the team had great parents, and those parents always helped me out: rides to the games and rides home, meals, a place to stay, encouraging words after a tough loss, advice on how to improve my game.

Objectively, Coach C had an extra ticket and he thought of me. I know it wasn't his intention that I would begin examining basketball existentially that night in May 1989. With Bird sitting there having to watch the team that kicked his ass more than any other team—Bill Laimbeer's strangleholds, Dennis Rodman's hip checks—I wondered what he was thinking. Bird would endure more injuries for a couple more years and finally retire in 1992. I felt edified by Bird's bone spurs. Bird was not going to play forever, and neither was I. What would I do when I stopped playing basketball? It was a question I never wanted to answer. The answer was bleak. Basketball was pointless; in the end it breaks you, and worse, you might have to wear a protective boot.

Larry sat there in street clothes with a protective boot on. I sat there underwhelmed. Here I was at my first Celtics game, high in the hallowed Garden seats, and I was bored. I didn't pay much attention to the game. The Pistons manhandled the Celtics that night. Detroit would go on to win the NBA championship that year and the following year.

When people asked me if I played college ball, I would hesitate and then want to say, "I could have, but . . ." But then I would sound like *that guy*. I could have continued playing in college, but I saw it as postponing the inevitable more than continuing something that I loved. So we broke up. It was an imperfect split. I probably broke up with her too early. I didn't want to be part of that couple that doesn't know how to finish the relationship, and so continues it long after its death. We left each other after I graduated from high school. I moved to Boston and college, she stayed in New Hampshire. Like most high school relationships, we left things open just in case. I was unable to stop loving her. It didn't end the way I had imagined. In 1993, I was supposed to be named New Hampshire's Mr. Basketball. I was also supposed to win a state championship my senior year. I was supposed to play college basketball. Basketball had meant so much—it had kept me in school, it forced me to be a better student—but I needed to pivot away. I needed to break the jock shell that basketball had encased me in.

I blame John Updike for scaring the poop out of me. One day in the library, I picked up a book. Truthfully, I was attracted to it only because it had a basketball on the cover. *Rabbit, Run.*

It was the line "If you have the guts to be yourself, other people'll pay your price" that turned my world upside down. If the passion of basketball transcends time, then one moment of pain could cancel an eternity of happiness. That last game hurt. I had worked hard over the four years to be the best player in New Hampshire. It didn't happen. Everyone knows high school love stories do not last long. (Except teenagers.) Logic and reason are useless against love. Who has the ability to extinguish the fire of a hoop dream? John Updike does, that's who.

Of course, I still love basketball. Yet it made me very unsophisticated; it prevented me from discovering the larger world we live in. Too much time was spent perfecting an imperfect jump shot. When you play too much basketball, you live in an underworld, a circle constructed of social and racial stratifications, political realities, and economic circumstances. It is inhabited by insipid journalists, sebaceous recruiters, corrupt officials, selfish players, diabolical agents, pedestrian parents, nefarious administrators, blind referees, vacuous fans, and washed-up former players. Maybe it's basketball's fatal charm that allures us like a mouse to a mousetrap. The desire to improve your handle or left hand engenders hunger for more cheese, and in the end we all get snared. Traveling through basketball's sphere of influence illuminates its tragedies, but unfortunately those cautionary tales do nothing to pry us from its sweet embrace. As soon as I was finished playing high school basketball, I became deeply concerned I would turn into another Rabbit Angstrom: cursed to be defined by my limited basketball prowess and to live the rest of my life selling vegetable peelers and bragging about what I accomplished on the hardwood when I was eighteen. I fought against that sealed fate and gave up the game. Now I've come full circle, and because of Coach C I'm back coaching the game I ran away from.

In 1998, after graduating from college, I traveled around Europe alone. Coach C had retired and was living in Geneva with his girlfriend. We were both starting something new. In 2003, when I started teaching, he sent me lesson plan outlines. In 2006, when I started coaching, Coach C sent me packages stuffed with hundreds of drills. In 2009, when my daughter Nina was born, he called to invite us to his house in Florida. Years after I had stopped playing, he was still in my life.

On March 27, 2014, I took my family to my high school alumni game. Coach C was there, and before him was his basketball diaspora. There were more than fifty of his former players. Teams were divided up by year of graduation: odd years to the left, even years to the right. It was a little confusing at first because both teams wore red T-shirts that read "Coach C's Alumni Game." Some of us ran, some of us trotted, a few walked up and down the court. We all had one eye on the ball and the other on the man who enhanced our adolescence and altered our lives.

Coach C transformed a lot of lives in southern New Hampshire, and no exhibition game, no eulogy, can begin to explain what he did. I went to the bench exhausted. My eyes were fixed on a kid in his twenties. He was faster and quicker than anyone else on the court, but I realized we all kind of played the same. It was as if we had Coach C in our basketball DNA. We had absorbed his fundamentals into our genes. We all had the same defensive stance, our follow-throughs looked eerily similar, we threw bounce passes that were mirror images of each other.

We had changed. A few of us were bald, many were gray, others I simply didn't recognize. I heard names that meant something once upon a time. It was one of those moments in basketball that transcend mere sport. We were there to play in front of Coach one last time as cancer ate at him. He sat, wheelchair bound, with a Red Sox jacket and a black-striped heather scarf wrapped around him. He would die only a few short weeks later. In some grand way, it was better than a funeral. He was alive. We joked, smiled, and cried at the same time. He patted Nina on her head and said, "You look like your dad." Laughing, with tears in our eyes, we wished he would yell at us and make us run suicides until we puked. We would have. His world was disappearing and ours was expanding. The bleachers were filled with our wives and kids watching their dads play.

I spoke to his longtime girlfriend, Ludmilla. The sight of her wheeling a man she had had a relationship with for almost two decades was painful. She stood there in deep sadness with her exhausted beauty. In Russian she said to me, "This has been so difficult for me." The last time I had seen the two of them was in Geneva in 1998. We spoke occasionally. We didn't speak enough.

Coach C was a teacher, a basketball coach, the father of two daughters. He loved Russian history and literature, and he was an author. I wondered if he knew how much we had in common. I wanted him to know this prima donna had become a *primo uomo*. I am now the man he hoped I would become when he brought me to the Celtics game when I was fifteen. I had created my own championship teams in New York City. I borrowed his effective full-court press and allegiance to team basketball. (I left behind some of the torture techniques and name-calling.) I am raising my daughters to be altruistic and urbane because of him. I think of him often. Coach C died, but he did what all great coaches are supposed to do: make sure his legacy lives inside his players.

THE BRONX

Derry, New Hampshire, is about 225 miles from the Bronx. You can say they are worlds apart, yet the game remains the same: five on five, four eight-minute quarters, ten-foot hoops, same rules. In gyms across New York City, similar tryouts like ours were unfolding, and you would never know that the Bronx is where one-quarter of the adults are obese, 10 percent have diabetes, and the rates of mental illness hospitalization and asthma deaths are some of the highest in the nation.

The Bronx is surrounded by and separated from its wealthy neighbors in Riverdale, Westchester County, and Manhattan. We are within the jurisdiction of the 42nd Police Precinct; to the south, the 40th Police Precinct, where a lot of our students live, has the second-highest homicide rate in New York City. Basketball is a sanctuary that allows us to forget about the issues outside. It's a lot more fun to think about how to beat a full-court press than it is to think about getting mugged going home from tryouts. This is the reality of living in the Bronx.

When was this Maginot Line formed? It is quite easy to diagnose when the Bronx started to change. It was in 1946, when Robert Moses proposed to build the Cross Bronx Expressway, a seven-mile highway that scythed a borough in half and screwed up the Bronx like no other urban planner could. This is well-known history, yet almost seventy years after Moses reshaped the Bronx, it still suffers colossally. Thanks in part to Moses's myopic vision and the institutional racism it engendered, the borough has long suffered from poverty, crime, and ill health, though in recent years there have been numerous efforts to correct this injustice.

The Bronx has the vastness of the Grand Concourse. On one corner I can see the hordes of *abuelas,* with their rickety shopping carts waiting in line in front of churches or food pantries. I see an *abuelo* still hurting after last night's loss at dominoes. The eye-catching belt buckles suggest the inverse of John Kenneth Galbraith's idea of public wealth and private squalor. I spot guys in their twenties smoking marijuana way too early in the day. Vacant synagogues of an ancient Bronx stand next to storefront *masjids,* projecting a new future.

I am a basketball junkie. There have been many times when I promised I would quit, but I can't. That probably doesn't mean anything to most people, but it means a lot to the young men I coach. I have committed the rules to heart, love the history, can diagram the swing offense, the Princeton offense, the flex, Frank Morris's numbered fast break, and dozens of out-of-bounds plays. Basketball may be just a game to some, a meaningless sport, a waste of time, a dream unfulfilled, but it keeps New Yorkers occupied year-round. There are thousands of basketball courts in New York City. There is no city in the world that has more rims without nets and basketball dreams than New York City.

It's not difficult to understand how important basketball is in New York City. Its character is not determined by the status of the Knicks or the Nets, who play an ersatz version of basketball. It is painful to watch a lone man endlessly dribbling the ball until the shot clock dwindles, and then launch an impossible shot. This happens a lot. Once a Mecca, the city is now Constantinople, the sick man of basketball cities. This is our nightmare.

My basketball sanctuary exists in that tiny gym in the Bronx. When I first started coaching, I wanted to know how I could be the best. It was a simple question. The game within the game is not about competition so much as it is how you can make your teammates better. Better cuts lead to better passing, more passing leads to more scoring, more scoring leads to more wins, more wins lead to better friendships. This is a longitudinal project. I believe I can text, email, or call anybody I played with in high school because we won together. I am not sure I could do that if we hadn't won more than we lost. That's why I love team ball and have no patience for anything else.

Each season we try to be the paragon of playing basketball the right way. You get to see multiple guys scoring in double digits; that and a few other elements are central to our success. Years ago, I researched the past PSAL champions and discovered the majority of those teams had four guys in double digits. You also need a team that cuts hard to the basket and passes the ball on time and on target. Another overlooked part of any team is the bench. The bench claps and cheers the whole game. The bench is a window into a team's soul. Kenneth, Bryant, Mack, Cris, and Kaleb do not stop clapping for their teammates, and when Frankie, Charles, Jaelen, Tyree, Shamar, and Walfri are on the bench they return the favor. We take good shots. We reverse the ball and find open teammates on kick-outs flawlessly. We get back on defense on every possession. In this city, in our time, the pro game and college game take a backseat to the high school games and players.

FIRST YEAR: 2003

When I began teaching at Fannie Lou Hamer Freedom High School in 2003, I was a flaneur. I didn't understand what was needed to help the young people I taught. My path was purely functional at first; I needed a job. But what started as a job while I was in graduate school transformed into a personal journey. Coaching became my compass.

One thing is clear to me now: get to know your students as best as you can. That wasn't always the case. On my very first day of teaching, I announced I was going to give a test.

"Mister, I don't take tests," a young girl told me.

Now wait a minute. In grad school we were taught we needed to test children to know what they know. Tests were like taking vital signs. We needed to know the baseline. Well, what if the test actually doesn't show you what the kid knows? Nobody had told me there are other ways for kids to show you what they know and how they think. My time in the Bronx has shown me over and over again that children learn from each other. Once a child trusts you, you can teach them anything from computer science to Russian literature. Teaching in the Bronx has become my Yale and my Harvard. Teachers need to be comedians, intellectuals, waiters, despots, psychologists, coaches in the classroom. We need to be empathetic and academically demanding. How does one motivate the unmotivated? How do we provide a challenging curriculum yet be careful not to crush the struggling students and to create independence in the classroom? As I was told by Nancy Mann, the former principal of Fannie Lou, "A teacher's persistence must outlast a student's resistance." You never give up.

One of my first assignments as a high school teacher was to

see where it all starts. Nancy sent me to observe a kindergarten class at Central Park East 1 Elementary School in Harlem. It altered me in ways I have trouble explaining. Watching five-year-olds work independently and cooperatively, I saw my ideal classroom. It would soon become my ideal basketball practice and later would affect the way I parent. Kids learn a lot from each other. To be honest, I'm horrible at collaborating, but I wanted my classroom to look like this, I wanted my team to look like this. I wanted my family someday to look like this classroom. I want society to work like this.

THE TROJAN HORSE THEORY OF BASKETBALL

As a coach, I have had some success on the hardwood, having won 199 games in eleven seasons, but my most important statistic comes in the classroom. In a city where the average graduation rate for black and Latino males is somewhere around 50 percent, 100 percent of my players have graduated, with 100 percent college placement. What's the secret to our success on and off the court?

It's simple. It's called trust.

In coaching it is said over and over again that the players don't care how much you know until they know how much you care. There is only one way to get trust, and that is by spending time with someone. We all know time is the ultimate limited resource. The calculus goes something like this: time plus trust equals love.

When I see Luis Kulan walking across the street, it makes me happy. I hadn't seen Luis in a few years. He was a reserve on the

2013 championship team. Right away he tells me, "I still talk to Mike, Corey, and Jimeek all the time," naming former players on the team. "I told my mom my son is going to come here. He's in second grade now."

His son, who looks just like Luis, stood there dribbling a ball that had been bleached from the sun. His white tank top revealed a small scab on his right shoulder. It looked similar to the ones I used to get when I would fall off my bike at his age.

"You know, Coach, I wouldn't have graduated if it wasn't for you and basketball. You remember? Sophomore year I was failing a bunch of classes and you made me get serious about school."

Luis was now a dental assistant at a local hospital.

"I want to stop by and see a game this year."

"I will send you a schedule," I promised.

"Thanks, Coach."

"Anytime, Luis."

Luis got me thinking. So I sent Jimeek Conyers, the starting point guard on the 2013 team, a text: "How did basketball help you?"

"If it wasn't for basketball I wouldn't even come to school," Jimeek responded.

"Without basketball would you have graduated?" I asked.

"Hell no!" Jimeek emphasized. "For real though, it made me want to come to school. It made me have a bond with people around the school. I hated school, but as I played more I started having bonds with people. Like I even got cool with the principal."

My idea was never just to create a winning basketball tradition. I was a teacher first, coach second. I believe that winning forms the necessary bonds to ask teenage boys with very little desire to come to school, to have a selfless spirit. There's no other way. Many of my guys have had little success in the classroom, and for years success on the court transfers into the classroom. Unfortunately, in almost two decades of teaching I've had to battle against the tentacles that poverty attaches to children. As a coach, I have figured out a way to transform lives with basketball. When you grow up poor, you quickly realize basketball can be a temporary relief from life as well as a motivating factor.

I asked Shateek Myrick, another former player, what basketball meant to him.

"Basketball always motivated me with school because I knew if I didn't meet a certain GPA I couldn't play, so it always pushed me through all my years of school."

Shateek graduated high school at twenty years old. He entered Fannie Lou as a sixteen-year-old freshman, played three years, and was ineligible his final year due to age restrictions. The odds of a sixteen-year-old black male graduating in four years are extremely low. I'm proud of Shateek. He enrolled at Cayuga Community College in the fall of 2017.

We know that high school dropouts earn less and live shorter, poorer, more complicated lives than those with a diploma. The young men I coach aren't good enough to play professional basketball, but that doesn't stop them from dreaming that one day they could. While they are playing and dreaming about basketball, the staff at Fannie Lou Hamer Freedom High School is preparing them for a world after basketball. Over the years it seems to be working, against the odds.

In ancient Troy, the horse was a sacred entity. So is basketball in the Bronx. The horse was also a ruse that the Greeks used to defeat the Trojans, and so are hoop dreams. My Trojan Horse Basketball Theory works like this: The boys welcome basketball into their sometimes stressful lives as a gift. They want to be part of the winning tradition at Fannie Lou. It looks like an innocuous present. Yet inside this synthetic leather ball game lie lessons in accountability, commitment, nutrition, civic responsibility, and a shot at self-actualization. Teenagers can be blind to the myriad possibilities that exist in this world. Basketball, I've found, can be a means of opening their eyes.

As they wait for their basketball dreams to come true, a type of incubation happens. The boys become enraptured with the sneakers, new gear, game preparation, winning, highlights, film breakdowns, scouting reports, off-season workouts. At the same time, they are coming to school and doing their work, forming bonds with the people around them—other players, college and high school coaches, reporters, officials—and for the most part staying out of serious trouble. After four years of high school, the dreams of NBA glory usually fade, and they wake up with a decent GPA, a chance at getting into college, and an opportunity to improve their lives. The innocence of playing high school basketball circumvents some of the manifold temptations of the city: gang violence, truancy, crime, and drugs.

My former players are my first line of defense. I asked Jamaal Lampkin several years after he graduated if he thought basketball helped him through high school.

"Marc, why do you keep asking questions you know the answer to? Basketball is the reason I have a diploma. Basketball taught me time management and a whole lot of things. Honestly, I wake up on time because of Sunday practices."

He will never let me forget the time I wouldn't let him into practice because he was late. He was never late again. "Because if you are late you could get kicked off the team. Just like work. It got me ready for the real world." Jamaal now works in IT for Barclays.

In the early years of coaching, I had conversations like this: "What are you going to do after basketball?"

"I'm going to the NBA," declared a young man I'll call Terrence.

"Terrence, you are five-ten and don't even start here." I stated the simple facts.

"I might grow. There's still time. Males don't stop growing until they're nineteen."

"What happens if you don't grow another ten inches?"

"Coach, you're a dream crusher."

"I guess I am."

Terrence, like so many other young men, planned on making it to the NBA. Even though he knew the odds, the dream had been etched into his mind, and there wasn't space on his palette for alternatives. Youthful confidence is indomitable. Terrence is now a junior in college majoring in business administration. He no longer plays basketball.

So the question is, how do I prepare kids to play basketball, win games, win championships, and then expect them when their four years are up to give up the dream of playing in the NBA and prepare for life without basketball? Imagine wrestling a salmon out of a grizzly bear's mouth, simultaneously trying to convince him you have one already cooked, so he should just let it go and come sit at the table. I wrestle dreams out of kids' minds and try to give them goals.

The first person I tried this Trojan Horse Basketball Theory on was myself, unknowingly. Basketball was the vehicle that drove me to do well in high school. I had dreams of playing college basketball. Yet when it was time to go to college and play, I walked away from the sport. My freshman year in college was an adjustment. I missed the game. I attempted to get a work-study job in the gym, but the only work-study job I could find was stacking books in the library. That is where I discovered the *Natya Shastra*, the Bauhaus, Hieronymus Bosch, La Nouvelle Vague, and Henry Miller. It was a whole new world. Strangely, Miller led me to Dostoevsky. Unearthing and reading Dostoevsky was the closest I have come to nirvana. Dostoevsky moved me so much that I started teaching myself Russian.

When time ran out on my basketball career, I wasn't trying to change the sail in the middle of a storm. I was safely in the harbor of a university. This is the road I want to provide, not some glory-filled path, but a more realistic, honest way forward, because the game ends for all of us at some point.

I think the earlier a kid gets to see what life is like on a college campus, the better. I was thrilled when I learned that Tyree applied and won an award for a free academic enrichment program. He spent the 2016 summer at the University of Texas in Austin, all sponsored by Verizon. He loved it. The only problem was he wasn't able to play basketball. They orchestrated academic classes in the morning and field trips in the afternoon. On the last night, in the August Texas dusk, they were playing a game of "Man-hunt," a teenage version of hide-and-seek, and trying not to get caught, Tyree put his hand through a plate of glass. "My hand was black with blood," he said. The coagulated blood stained his shooting arm and caused a pronounced fear in the young man: Would he ever be able to play basketball again? Tyree confessed, "I started crying when I got by myself, and I was thinking my arm wouldn't be able to move the same. I had pains and everything, but once the stitches came out, then I was stretching a little and played through the pain." Now Tyree is fine.

When I stepped into the classroom seventeen years ago, I learned right away that you can't say, *Hey, just do like me, watch me, it's easy.* It's not easy. Life is not easy. Teaching in the south Bronx is challenging. I try to create trust with kids from difficult circumstances and move my players and students to become the best version of themselves against the odds. In the gigantic wind tunnel of the human experience, I am trying to extend my teaching and coaching into meaningful longitudinal relationships. And my vehicle—my Trojan Horse—is basketball.

THE TALE OF TWO FORWARDS

Sometimes the good intentions of basketball have unintended consequences. Early in the season, I will sometimes stay up late and watch some West Coast basketball. In an NBA preseason game, I saw some early offense from the Portland Trail Blazers that I liked. They were able to get their guards to post up on the weak side. This would be perfect for Charles Davis and Latrell Anderson, our two best athletes. They are best friends. They went to the same middle school and decided to come to Fannie Lou as a dynamic duo. When Charles was a freshman, he boasted that he would leave Fannie Lou as its all-time leading scorer. Now a junior, Charles is the best player on the team. Over the past two seasons he has been a paradigm of growth and dedication. Charles reminded me of Bill Russell, the great Celtics center. Russell blocked shots not only to intimidate, he blocked shots *to his teammates*. He kept the ball inbounds. That is Charles. Once I overheard a kid teasing him that he had only 15 points in a game. Charles calmly reminded him that we won. He cared only about winning. He had led the team in scoring and rebounding last year, and he looked stronger than the last time I saw him in June.

Latrell, on the other hand, had shown flashes of brilliance, but he was streaky and inconsistent. He was always the best shooter in practice. His strong shoulders formed two perfect, symmetrical ninety-degree angles with his head. He called himself "Chill-Balla." It was an apt nickname, because he never got upset. He was always the coolest guy in the room.

Each of the last two seasons, it always looked as if Latrell was ready to puncture the starting lineup. He did a few times, but then suddenly his ascension would be derailed by an asthma attack, a malfunctioning alarm clock, babysitting duty, a tooth-ache, a stomachache, a sprained ankle, or a family emergency. Last year he told me his sixteen-year-old cousin had been shot. This happened right before the playoffs. He would miss a few practices and be out of the rotation. He was always emerging, but never fully arriving. We could depend on Charles. We were counting on (but really hoping for) Latrell to be the starting small forward. His size—six-two—and his athleticism would give us a competitive edge.

When I got to school, I saw Kenneth Castro in the hallway. "Good morning, Coach."

I thought it was a bit presumptuous to assume I would be his coach since we still had a few more tryouts left, and Kenneth hadn't quite won me over with his basketball sorcery.

Kenneth Castro is about five-seven when he is wearing sneak-ers and if you include his amber-brown flat-top. He has the tan face and goatee of your favorite alternative band's bassist from the 1990s. The wispy goatee has been growing since eighth grade and hasn't been quite as prodigious as he would like; nonetheless, he has grand plans for it. Kenneth's baseline personality shifts between extremely polite and insanely polite.

"Can you clap and cheer for the team all season long?"

"Of course."

"What happens if you don't play for three or four games—will you come to practice?"

"Of course."

"What's your favorite team?"

"The Panthers."

"Good answer, but I meant in the NBA."

"Golden State."

"You see how everyone is always cheering for the guys on the floor, during a time-out they are high-fiving them, giving them positive vibes? Can you do that for us?"

"Yes!"

His Facebook profile page captured Kenneth's endearing quality. It read, "One of these days I will be a champion, either in high school, college, or the NBA." Kenneth fulfilled one criterion of what we needed to have: a mensch on the bench.

Later that day I entered the gym, and everyone was dressed and standing at half-court waiting for me. "Today is the last day of tryouts," Gaby warned everyone.

Gaby Acuria, warm and well liked by teachers and students, was my right-hand man. He helped the team immensely. After school Gaby assisted at practice, games, and scouting. During the school day he defused situations, ran interference, and intercepted more potential conflicts than a Patriots cornerback playing against the Jets. His permanent disposition was helpful. Gaby graduated from Fannie Lou in 2008. He is now a special education teaching assistant and paraprofessional. He is working toward his bachelor's degree.

We had used the remaining tryouts to stress communication. Gaby and I reminded the guys that you have to hustle on every possession. Some listened, but most were distracted. Before I got to the gym, they wanted to see who could jump the highest. There were smudged fingerprints left high above the rim on the pellucid backboard. I figured they had to be from Charles, Latrell, or Tyree, as nobody else could jump as high. Suddenly, our attention left the evidence on the Plexiglas and turned to the roof. Rain dribbled like marbles, operatically, on the tin roof.

"I guess we aren't going outside today." Their collective sigh filled the gym and was met with the solitary smirk I permanently wear on my face. "Let's watch a movie."

Relief filled their spirits. Instead of shooting layups or making outlet passes, we watched a film. They needed to know what we needed to do to compete. I decided it was time to watch last year's buzzer beater at Morris High School, a rainy-day movie with a happy ending. Plus, there was one last criterion to make the team: I wanted to see who could stay awake during the film.

The DeWitt Clinton season-opening game was a month away. It loomed larger on the calendar at the end of each day.

We settled into my classroom. The game was already on my desktop. I turned on the Smart Board while guys dragged chairs and moved into position.

"You have to hustle on every possession," I hear myself repeating to the team in a mise en abyme moment. It is like a dream within a dream. All my prior seasons are locked in this one. I can't separate them. I attempted to censor my own negative thoughts about last season's triumph, of a 26-3 record, but the loss in the semifinals still seemed like an ultimate failure.

On the screen there is a loose ball and multiple guys are diving on the floor. I paused the film for effect. Last year, it became obvious that we consistently outhustled teams. I write in my notebook now: "Outscore teams this year."

"What just happened?" Three Fannie Lou players were on the floor scrambling for a loose ball.

Watching last year's Morris game was like unspooling a dream. Expectations were high. But the memory of last season's semifinal loss still stung. The locker room after that game felt like a funeral. Last season seemed like a broken promise I needed to amend. Seasons are written in chalk in October. They are not tattooed until March.

I was eating breakfast the next day when I received an early text.

"Coach, I want to thank you for everything, but I can't play this year."

Xavier quit the team. How do I solve for X? I was surprised that he quit, but not shocked.

"X quit," I told Jess, my wife.

"Is he okay?" Jess asked compassionately.

I kissed Jess and Salome, my youngest daughter, good-bye. Nina, my oldest daughter, and I walked to the bus stop. The

October mornings are dark and cool. Nina got on the bus and found a seat near the window. She then made some funny faces at me, and as the bus pulled away she made a heart with her tiny hands. I pretended to race the bus. On Broadway the police were questioning a well-dressed man. Was he robbed? Was he the suspect? The light turned green.

I headed toward the High Bridge on my bike. This part of my ride to work was still a novel treat. I pretended I was riding into the woods. It's a short path, but the tree canopy was like a cocoon. I liked the smell of decaying leaves, and the cold morning air was making my nose run. The wet leaves on the path were also littered with acorns. Acorns cause flats. So does broken glass. The fear of getting a flat tire consumed most of my commute, but I couldn't forget about Xavier. The steel gates of the newly opened High Bridge were open, taking me from upper Manhattan to the Bronx. A man sat on a bench scratching lottery tickets while his white puppy thought about chasing me. I'm not upset when someone quits; it generally means they have found something outside basketball. You hope it is something positive. As a coach, I'm disappointed that we lost a starter; as a teacher, I think I've done something to get him at least to this point in his life.

This is the scene when you cross the High Bridge, the bridge that first sent potable water to thirsty Manhattanites in 1845. To my left is the twisting, clogged, descending intestines of the Cross Bronx slowly dumping commuters onto the Major Deegan. To my right is the skyline of Manhattan. The conspicuous, ultra-skinny towers of "oligarch's row" growing taller and taller. My bike rattled over the beige brick, the cuff of my new gray pants was now tattooed in black bike grease, and I thought: *Who sleeps in those synthetic obelisks pointing to the stratosphere?*

I maneuvered toward West 170th across Jerome Avenue and continued east on East 170th Street.

I hope X is okay.

A small tent city in a tunnel under the Grand Concourse has
a few more residents than I remembered. The smell of urine and
feces was overwhelming. "The Ballad of Reading Gaol," Oscar
Wilde's prison poem, came to my mind:

Each narrow cell in which we dwell
Is a foul and dark latrine,
And the fetid breath of living Death
Chokes up each grated screen,
And all, but Lust, is turned to dust
In Humanity's machine.

As I exit from the tunnel underneath the Grand Concourse,
I can hear trumpets and cowbells. "Salsa Buena" by Frankie
Ruiz y la Solucion. The distance from Anglo-Irish poets to
Caribbean salsa is never too far in the Bronx. The poem and
the music clashed in my head. I pedaled across Morris Avenue.
I avoided the trucks delivering bread to the supermarket. The
11 bus softened the sound of the collisions of the claves while
the rhythm of the guiros and maracas moved my legs. My shoes
are clipped into my pedals. I guess that is kind of how I dance,
glued to the floor. Here I was climbing up 170th Street, and I
find the source: a small speaker attached to a shiny purple bike.
The tires are thick with whitewall. A banana seat never looked
more comfortable.

Two days later Luis, after eight years as my assistant, informed
me he would not be able to commit to the season.
   I guess my mixture of authoritarianism and humanitarianism
needed to be recalibrated. Were these departures coincidental?
I think it revealed that I have become the guardian of the
program, and to keep it alive and functioning required setting
standards. If it was simply a forum for anyone to come and
go as they pleased, we wouldn't win games. Truth is, winning

matters above everything because it binds us, builds trust and friendships.

Still, I started to question my motives. Was the season over before it started? Was it time to stop coaching? I could hear the sounds of salsa echoing in this prison I had created.

Then Xavier found me in the gym.

"Coach, you know I can graduate in January, and I don't think it is fair to the team if I stay only to leave halfway through the season." Xavier was emotionally torn. He didn't want to quit, but he had earned enough credits and would meet all the graduation requirements early. Plus, he wanted to find a job. He had a lot on his plate.

"I want you to play, but I understand," I told him. "Thank you for all your hard work and dedication to the team."

BRIAN IS MISSING

It was a bittersweet ending for Xavier. I was looking forward to his leadership and guidance. A young team had suddenly become a lot younger. I was in my classroom after school, thinking about how we could win with such a young team. Can Walfri, Bryant, and Charles control the paint? Can Mack and Frankie be our primary ball handlers? Will Shamar, Latrell, and Tyree shoot well enough from the wings to keep us competitive? I knew we could play defense. The freshmen Kaleb, Jaelen, and Brandon will be brought along slowly. My room was so quiet. Schools without children seem haunted.

I was about to go home, when my sister Jennifer sent me a text telling me to look at my brother's Facebook posts. I have had a fear for a long time that my brother would die on the day of a game.

The next message came in before I could respond.

"Brian is missing. He said he was going to kill himself."

I hate virtual suicide notes. I felt my madness madden. I felt my sadness sadden. Brian, my younger brother, has had a lifelong dependency on drugs. This was his latest heist, a social media hijack that would send everyone running to the comments section to rescue him. "Help . . ." he wrote. Then signed off. Xavier's loss to the team was manageable. This was something else.

When I ran away from home at sixteen, it left my brother, Brian, eleven at the time, and my sister Jennifer, eight, right in the middle of the fire. Brian would start smoking marijuana at thirteen. He would drop out of school when he was fifteen. He would injure his back as a laborer when he was twenty-two. He would first take OxyContin for the pain, then a few years later he was hooked on heroin. Sound familiar?

Brian's actions always alarmed my mom the most. Of course, this message sent her on a rescue mission in the shadows of the White Mountains. She looked in granite quarries, near lake shores and streambeds, the same way parents look for an abducted child: frantic, imagining the worst, crippled by the unknown, praying. I imagined a gorgeous September day in northern New Hampshire (the state has the second-highest overdose rate in the nation, behind West Virginia) with leaves starting to turn blood-orange, brilliant yellow, deep red, a chill in the morning, and my panicked mom short of breath, a lifelong smoker, yelling and screaming and crying for her thirty-seven-year-old son among the red maples, paper birch, and evergreen pines. Brian was somewhere, unable to take the pain of his life but brave enough to announce to the world he was done with us.

Later that day Jen, the hero in our family, drove after work, without dinner, to find our despondent mom in a hotel. The next day they would canvass the town, chauffeured by sympathetic police officers. They told my mom they do this a lot. They showed Diane all the spots where the junkies hang out, like she was on a tour of celebrity homes in California. Can a mom recover if she sees her son dead in the woods? Diane's life has been very difficult. Her parents died when she was young. She is estranged from her sisters. Her younger brother is in prison for life. Drugs and alcohol became her extended family. Would finding her dead son be her final misfortune? The crushing grief? For nearly all my adult life, my mother has been sober. Would this push my mom to start using again? She's fragile. She has been battling her own demons. When I finally talked to my mom, her hysteria had turned to anger.

"He needs to pull his pants up and act like a man."

"Mom, he doesn't need a lecture now," Jen said. Always caught in the middle, Jen would plead with her to relent.

I was always too far away from the epicenter of their dysfunction to ever really feel the aftershock. Hours went by. Then Brian went back to his device and announced that he would now finish the job. I imagined he was trying to make threats to read the sympathetic pleas, and then his phone died. Where did he go now to charge his phone? How can he continue to torture the world with his suicidal threats? Does he realize his sons will someday read his posts?

He had told the world, at least those who follow him on Facebook, that he was molested at camp when he was seven. He said he lost his brother (me), his hero, when he was eleven. He couldn't find his parents when he needed food. He picked his inebriated mom off the floor and put her to bed. His wife cheated on him with his best friends. He stole an inheritance from his new girlfriend.

Recently I see he got a neck tattoo of a Celtic cross. I don't think he has ever been to church. Heroin, like any pursuit, eventually destroys the unconquerable whole. Brian was falling to pieces again.

My mother and sister found him the following morning.

Jen told me about the girl behind the counter at Dunkin' Donuts in Littleton. She was wearing a green and gray Plymouth State sweatshirt, looking as if she knew she never should have dropped out of college. Once she quit, she knew she would be stuck for life making light and sweet coffee for all the other people in this small town. She had memorized her customers and their legal addiction to caffeine and sugar. I was told the heartbroken moms of the heroin trade frequently visited this coffee shop asking the pretty cashier with auburn hair and a splash of freckles across her cheeks if she had seen their missing scions. The pictures on their phones were of familiar faces. Not that she really knew them; they were the new daily customers. Heroin has a way of making everyone look related. The parents' hands always shook. She developed a habit of taking the phone, especially from the dads, to save them the embarrassment of their predicament. She held the phone close, delicately, so she could see the child before the heroin had eaten the adipose tissue from their face and destroyed them. She promised to call the police as soon as she saw them. Moms leaned awkwardly across the counter to hug her. Rheumy dads nodded with deep pride and approval.

When the Wanted or the Missing ordered a coffee, she would feign that she was out of cream, go into the back room, and call the police. She was used to genuflecting parents thanking her. The police were happy they had a set of eyes and a member of the community who was trying to help with the opioid epidemic.

Then the cops arrived and found my brother. He tilted his head, pursed his lips at the clerk, and slowly said, "Oh, that's why you disappeared and said there was no more cream."

Jen handed the phone to my mom.

"You feeling okay, Mom?"

"Yeah, I'm just glad I know where he is now." A familiar phrase worried parents everywhere have said.

My mom asked, "How's the team doing?"

PART TWO

REGULAR SEASON

NOVEMBER

Each November I reread the opening paragraph from *Moby-Dick*. November is not just the time of the year when Ishmael was about to walk down the streets and knock people's hats off. It is also high time for the season to get going. November must be the hardest month on coaches, because there's so much to do: implement an offense, or reintroduce help-side defense like a forgotten foreign language. November is when I need to be in the gym running practices, screaming about abstract intangibles and invisible stats, or preparing my team to knock someone's head off from a pulpit. Coaching produces this feeling: a fusion of helplessness, anticipation, and total frustration. It's a mix of sacrificial devotion and extreme confidence, laced with an asymmetrical sarcasm heading down a one-way street toward the younger generation, who may or may not feel as passionate as you do about the game.

Practices officially started in November. The team was set. We finally had a quorum. We were confident the new guys Cris, Brandon, Kenneth, Jaelen, and Kaleb would contribute during their maiden basketball season. We were also counting on the returning guys: Walfri, Shamar, Jaquan, Bryant, Latrell, Charles, Frankie, and Tyree. Thirteen guys made up the squad: three freshmen, three sophomores, five juniors, and two seniors. Were we any good? I thought we might be really good, except we weren't any good. We were too young, too turnover-prone, and lacked serious depth.

Maybe next year, I thought. The utility of canning was never more obvious. This novitiate of a basketball season, like all seasons, would be difficult: any trip or journey was a course in self-discipline. It was also a period of purposeful self-deception; over the next few months, we would have to really improve to win a championship.

It is not trivial to state we were a young team. I've carried just two seniors before—that was the *Long Hardwood Journey* season. We won fifteen games and lost in the first round of the playoffs. Yet it could be possible we had the right mixture of young and old, hardworking upperclassmen with something to prove and soon-to-be-prodigious sophomores. Were we too scarred from last season's loss, or was that even a crowbar I could use with this team? I tried to sketch the outline of the 2016–17 team, but it was like stenciling a jellyfish. Would we float around all season harmlessly, or would we be terrifyingly aggressive and shut down beaches? I wasn't sure.

THE 2016 ELECTION

On the subject of uncertainty, the presidential election was in two days. My father-in-law kept sending me emails that Trump was going to win and this was what Berlin was like in 1932. I already missed Obama. He deported more people than any president before him, ordered more people killed with drones, and has concealed volumes of hidden secrets. I'll miss being misled by him.

The first day of practice had been on a Sunday. The youthfulness was palpable on the team; seniors usually cast a cloud of seriousness. The underclassmen gave off the faux impression of knowing the core values that we embrace: mental toughness, selflessness, guarded optimism, a determination to improve, and commitment to the team. Only Latrell and Brandon were absent. Sunday practices form the bedrock of the season. We usually start around ten a.m. and finish around two p.m. Frankie looked unstoppable on both sides of the ball. I wanted Charles to defend him, but I needed Charles and Walfri to challenge each other today. So I placed them against each other. Practices were going to be a little uneven until I figured out a way to balance the drills.

I woke up Wednesday morning earlier than usual. I poked my phone awake.

"How 'bout them apples?" a text from my sister read.

We woke up on that first Wednesday in November and found out Donald Trump was the president-elect. I wish it had been about apples.

At school, there was a deep malaise. Everyone showed signs of being concussed.

"Hillary Clinton won the election," some students announced awkwardly; she was the winner of the school-wide mock election.

"Who cares?" I heard someone yell in the hallway. I stepped deeper into a certain adult sadness I have never felt. I heard a teacher compare the feeling to 9/11.

The students were shocked. There was talk of walls being built, the death of the Black Lives Matter movement, deportation. The texts I received from the guys on the team, former and current, are telling:

"I thought it was a dream until I looked it up. Damn." (Dalen Ward, a manager)

"I was frozen with fear." (Travis Peterson, class of 2016)

"I'm disappointed because I am under the category he is against." (Dan Findley, class of 2014)

"I thought to myself that my family would want to move

to the Dominican Republic because Trump hates immigrants."
(Kenneth Castro)

"I wondered if my parents would let me go live with my
grandparents in Belize." (Jaelen Bennett)

By Friday, a section of the hallway became a community message board. Taped to the wall was a sign on violet paper that
read YOU ARE LOVED. Underneath it, printed on electric emerald,
aquamarine, fuchsia, and canary yellow paper in bold font and
black ink, were other mitigating posters: DEAR UNDOCUMENTED
STUDENTS, AT THIS SCHOOL THERE ARE NO WALLS. And so on.

Basketball became a sanctuary from the madness of this election. The Clinton (no relation) opening game was only two days
away. I tried to bury myself in basketball. Trump's election didn't
make sense to most of the people I knew.

Game day arrives, and I have a bit of a confession: on game
day I always get terrified right before I wake up. That place
that we occupy right before we awake has me convinced I have
forgotten how to coach: not sure how many time-outs I have,
whom to sub in or out, who we are playing, will I get the team
lost on our way there, do I have enough MetroCards, is it even
an away game tonight or is it home, what out-of-bounds plays
do we run against a 2–3 zone? I forget the names of our plays.
I see myself standing clueless, paralyzed; never mind the extinct
playbook and the extant players, my mind is a tabula rasa. A
few years ago, to avoid slipping into this fictional paralysis, I
started carrying a cheat sheet for every game the way Pushkin
always carried two revolvers; it has all our man-to-man and
zone plays and code words: green for pick-and-roll, yellow for
pick-and-pop, gray for a dribble handoff. Once the game starts,
I rarely need it; it sits quietly on a clipboard under my chair.
But all day the fear sits with me. When I eat my breakfast I
wonder if I was obeying the right superstition: I grew a beard,
trimming underneath my jaw once a week on Sundays, along

with my little bit of hair that occupies my head. How bad will the refs suck tonight, I wonder. The fear stays with me during warm-ups. The pregame handshake is when it finally disappears.

GAME ONE VERSUS DEWITT CLINTON

On a crowded 4 train I was thinking about last year's opener against Morris High School, the oldest high school in the Bronx. Years ago, I read about it in Jonathan Kozol's *Savage Inequalities,* where he placed the school in "a landscape of hopelessness—burnt-out apartments, boarded windows, vacant lot upon garbage-strewn vacant lot" surrounding it. Now it is called the Morris Educational Complex. It has rebounded well. It is no longer a large comprehensive school, but a campus that has four separate high schools: School for Violin and Dance, Bronx International, School for Excellence, and Morris Academy for Collaborative Study. The inside looks totally different; Kozol should return. But truthfully, I was more concerned about how we were going to beat Morris without Charles, who'd been briefly suspended for some corridor horseplay, than about what Kozol would say.

"Hey, next stop." Gaby broke my spell and that of some sleepy commuters and alerted us from his crow's nest.

"There it is," Shamar confirmed.

Shamar knew every school and basketball court in the city. It was fun to travel with him. We walk into gyms in Brooklyn or in Chelsea, and everyone says what's up to him. It's a double homage: they are recognizing his game and that he is such a friendly guy that he has dudes all over the city acknowledging him.

Coaching Shamar is a pleasure. He displays such docile obedience that he answers, "Yes, Coach" with an almost military acquiescence that makes me a little uncomfortable. I had expected outlawry. His first two years he would come to try out and ran around like a caffeinated squirrel. I didn't think I could coach him. His junior year was his apprenticeship or residency. Now in his senior year, he would be the attending surgeon on the floor. His silence wasn't resistance; it was maturity and trust. He was charming, like a postcard from an old friend.

He had moved often when he was younger. He even left the city because of family issues for a while and lived in places as far away as Kentucky. Such things clearly shaped, changed, and inspired him. Everywhere we went *everyone* knew Shamar. Not because he had lived all over the city, but because he had played in playgrounds and leagues all over the city. He was at home at every court in New York City. If they didn't know Shamar, they knew his twin brother, Zaire, who played basketball at Lehman High School.

It is common for high school boys to be absentminded, and Shamar was no exception. He was blessed with amazing speed and a smooth jump shot, but they came with teenage forgetfulness. Still, he was quick to apologize when he committed a turnover, and even quicker to correct the mistake on defense; a steal, a deflection, or a rebound usually followed. Shamar said, "Every time I made a bad pass I would try to get a steal on the next possession." It was an honorable exchange. I love to coach kids like Shamar.

Beyond the trees and between a large high-rise apartment, we could see the mammoth DeWitt Clinton High School looming in the distance. We descended the Mosholu Parkway Station stairs. The sun set over the acres the Dewitt Clinton High School campus occupies.

"Yo, look at this place," I heard someone say.

"It's like a hundred times bigger than our school."

The entrance was protected by a barrier of steel scaffolding. We entered the ziggurat and lined up to go through the school's scanning devices. Then we were instructed to take off our belts and remove any loose change and cell phones from our pockets. Next we were told to empty our change into a white plastic basket. I felt an ecclesiastical pregame ritual unfolding.

"I feel like I'm already guilty when I walk through these," Frankie said.

"I'm glad Fannie Lou doesn't have them," Shamar confessed.

Clinton High School is the high church of the Public Schools Athletic League, with eighteen players in the NBA and two in the Hall of Fame: Tiny Archibald and Dolph Schayes. We were in a veritable armory of basketball luminaries. This city has produced some of the world's most talented shooters, dunkers, passers, and dribbling maestros, and Clinton was the cradle for some of the city's best. Johnny Most, the voice of the Boston Celtics, graduated from here. New Hampshire had only one guy, Mark Bonner, ever make it to the NBA; New York City has had more than three hundred. Everywhere I went, greatness had been: Stevenson High School, home of Ed Pinckney; Rice High School, home of Kemba Walker, Dean Meminger, and Felipe Lopez; La Salle, home of Ron Artest; Boys High, home of Connie Hawkins; Xaverian, home of Chris Mullin; Archbishop Molloy, home of Kenny Anderson and Kenny Smith; Andrew Jackson High School, home of the legendary Bob Cousy. Starting out, I wasn't as truly awestruck by the significance of New York City basketball as I should have been. The idol worship meant little to me. I wanted to get up to the gym and start the season off with a win.

This was also Gaby's first time in the cathedral where the ancient running track sat above the court like a dimmed halo. He predicted, "This game is going to be just like the Morris game last year."

As we waited for the rest of the team and their items to be X-rayed, a young school safety officer asked if we were playing the JV or the varsity team tonight. We said the varsity.

"I hope you're ready," he said, smiling, as if he already knew the results based on our inability to get through the scanning process quickly.

I bit my lip. "I hope so too."

A Clinton player appeared in the lobby, a little upset that his girlfriend wouldn't be allowed to go to the game. We were invisible to him. He seemed more concerned with how many people were there to see him than with the opposing team waiting in the lobby.

I whispered to Gaby, "Is everyone in here not expecting us to win?"

"The players are worried about getting their fan club in."

"How much did they beat Lab Museum High School by?" Gaby asked.

"Thirteen," I said.

"They just activated some football players too."

Inside the belly of the leviathan, the monastic blue walls were unadorned. We must have been so busy talking about how big the school was that we got lost in the labyrinth. We were given directions to the gym after a long walk down a hallway. We took a left and were now deep inside the Clinton catacombs. We kept walking until we came to a passageway, where we repeated the directions aloud. We were now really lost in this cavernous underbelly. "Imagine if you get caught lacking?" Mack wondered aloud what might happen if they ran into the wrong dudes at the wrong time.

"Even Jackson couldn't find us here," Josh Emanuel, the

scorekeeper, said, referring to our own school safety agent, the intrepid Ms. Jackson. It was funny that she was on their minds as we walked down the hall of another school. It was also a sign of how meaningful she is to our school and how safe they feel at Fannie Lou, even without metal detectors. So the feeling of going through a metal detector at each away game usually brings up new emotions for the guys on the team.

We took another set of stairs and entered what we thought was the gym. Instead of a basketball court, we walked into a gymnastics practice.

"Upstairs," a kid on the uneven bars instructed us.

"They have two gyms? Get outta here," Charles said in disbelief.

"Not gonna lie, this place is huge," Frankie exclaimed.

We eventually found the gym.

The Clinton Governors were warming up. Their players mirrored the school in size: they were bigger, stronger, and older. Even the music was louder than ours. I glanced up at the scoreboard. It looked as if it had seen better days. Lightbulbs were missing, and it was impossible to decipher fives from ones or sevens from eights. And for the encore, I see the referee, Mike Napolitano, who played on Clinton's championship team in 1977. The other ref could have still been a student at Clinton for all I knew.

We changed, as we always do, in a classroom. Jerseys and shorts flew in the air to their respected owner.

Walfri held number 33 in his hand and looked at me. "Where's Brandon?"

"He quit this morning."

"Why?"

"No idea."

Walfri shrugged and shoved the jersey back into the bag. Brandon told me he wanted to concentrate on school, and basketball was taking up a lot of his time. It was the first time

I have had someone quit the day of our first game. I scanned
the room and watched Jaelen, the other promising freshman,
remove his basketball medallion on a thin silver chain. His black
hair looked soft like an onyx sponge.

We head out to the gym. I can't get cozy with the opposing
coach before games. I am seeking to destroy his team, and he's
spent hours preparing to beat mine. It is a little disingenuous to
feign the pregame buddy charade. Chris Ballerini is the exception. He has coached and taught in the Bronx for as many years
as I have. We are part of the same tribe of coaches who love the
game and demand a lot from our players. Still, he wants to beat
me and I want to beat him.

"You have some big guys," I said.

"Yeah, just activated some football players. This guy is a
Division One lineman. He's probably going to go to Fordham.
He's a great athlete and good kid."

I might be able to activate Josh, my five-seven scorekeeper, in
February, if he improves his grades, I thought to myself.

Two former players, Timmy Hariston and Travis Peterson,
home from college on Thanksgiving break, walked into the gym.

"Travis, can you do the scorebook?"

"Of course. What's wrong with Josh?"

"Too green, and look at the scoreboard!"

"Yo, moe, what is that?" The illuminated zetas, lambdas, and
deltas appeared like Ptolemy's table of chords.

"Just make sure everyone at the table is keeping the correct
running score," I pleaded.

I scribbled instructions on the white clipboard with a pink
dry-erase marker. Then the buzzer sounded, announcing the
start of the 2016–17 season.

I outlined our defensive strategy against the flex offense.
"When they run flex, switch and stay in the paint right in front
of the rim." The flex offense is a series of predictable cuts and
screens that can generate a lot of layups and open jump shots.

"Watch when they run the Celtics out-of-bounds switch on all screens." Clinton's "Celtics" baseline out-of-bounds play looked like this: the four and five screen for the guards to take either an open three or a layup.

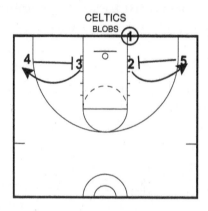

"Talk on defense." I took a deep breath.

"Let's make it a great season."

I probably unpacked a few more coaching clichés. I tried to fold them nicely and put them away before the game. We stretched our arms together to form a human temple of arms.

"One, two, three, Panthers, four, five, six, together!"

Walfri, Charles, and Frankie were returning starters. Shamar and Tyree, a sophomore, had been catapulted from the end of the bench into the starting lineup. Tyree was a natural runner, a Puerto Rican Prefontaine. At tryouts last year he effortlessly passed the older players on the track, lap after lap, drill after drill. He had outworked Latrell in the last few practices, and today he looked comfortable in the starting lineup. Charles won the tip on the first possession of the 2016–17 season. The ball moved from player to player with acuity, they made beautiful precise cuts to the basket, and for thirty-five seconds of the season we played quintessential team basketball. Until the horn sounded. On our first possession of the season, we forgot to shoot and received a thirty-five-second shot-clock violation.

A few possessions later, Frankie clawed a rebound, spotted Tyree running on his left, and floated a perfect outlet pass. Tyree with one dribble whipped the ball across his body to a wide-open Shamar on the right wing, *swish*. It was a beautiful catch-and-shoot for the first basket of the season. Tyree with the assist. Frankie with the hockey assist. They made it look effortless.

Later, Shamar said that shot was the most important shot of the season for him. "It gave me confidence," he confessed.

Our next and only other field goal of the first quarter came off of a patterned press-break. The Clinton defenders attempted to trap Charles in the corner, so he quickly pivoted and found a speeding Shamar. Shamar's speed, like Tyree's, was legendary. He dribbled toward the basket, and as a few white jerseys moved toward him Shamar made a no-look pass to Frankie in the paint for an easy layup. The first quarter ended with the score tied at 5–5. It was more like a baseball game going into extra innings than a New York City high school basketball game.

At some point in the first quarter, after another mindless turnover, tired of stomping my feet, I turned and kicked the wooden bench in frustration. I could see the Clinton principal, all six feet six inches of him, looming across the court. He was wearing a white shirt with a red tie, looking almost presidential. I imagined an unpleasant conversation with Jeff Palladino, the principal of Fannie Lou, the next day. The call never came.

The game was marred by horrendously bad shooting, and by kids taking too many steps with the ball. Walfri cut early and Frankie threw the ball into the stands. It was another ordinary chilly Monday evening in November, and Frankie looked at the scorer's table after his error and then at the bench with a look of disbelief. No substitutions. His head disappeared, his chin resting on his chest. This is not what he had worked all summer for, this moment is not why he traveled to Atlanta for a week of basketball camp, this moment he needed a substitution. I wasn't giving him one. "Get your damn head in the game. You are not coming out." More disbelief. "Of course they're making us turn it over. This is Clinton!" Usually you can see when a kid is trying hard not to be afraid; his eyes are dilated like an owl, he stops sweating. Frankie was beyond nervous. Frankie once told me that he scans the crowd and can always find his mom. "If she is not there, I don't play well. When she's there, I always feel fine. You know, it's like the one person in the world who loves me like no other." Most of my players are made in their mother's shade. If the father isn't around, the mothers try their best to provide for their sons.

I looked in the stands and couldn't find his mom. She would usually rush to every game after work. I had another irritant besides the mindless turnovers. On this hallowed court, my blue and black gingham button-up was having a hard time staying tucked in. I too was nervous and couldn't sit down, my sleeves were rolled up, I was pacing up and down. I looked over at Chris, who had removed his heather-gray sweater.

We started the second quarter with back-to-back-to-back unforced turnovers. I raked my face. Can jellyfish drown? The first half of the game was an invitation to play Twister in a tar pit. The halftime score was 13–12. Neither team could find any rhythm. A typical first game of the season.

I was hoping to swing the pendulum after halftime, but in the third quarter our guys looked winded and Clinton took control. Frankie was still shaky. Tyree was scoreless. Charles kept tap-dancing with his pivot foot: shuffle step, heel, spank, double cramp roll, travel. It was as impressive as it was illegal. So I went to the bench. After Brandon's departure I didn't want to frighten another freshman, so Jaelen remained on the bench. Could the juniors Jaquan and Latrell, who had been with me since they were freshmen, give us a spark? They entered to give Frankie and Tyree a break.

Clinton's size and the large crowd all seemed to wear us

down. The score was 31–27, I think (the worn-out byzantine scoreboard was difficult to read), at the end of the third quarter. Clinton had hit four three-pointers to push the lead up to four.

To start the fourth, Charles wrestled on the floor for a loose ball like a kitten with a ball of yarn. Jaquan corralled the ball. He zigzagged his way to initiate the offense. Latrell caught the ball on the right wing. He looked unsure of what to do, the way you hesitate for a second before you guess which line at the supermarket will be quicker. He decided to attack the basket, one dribble with his right hand and then a between-the-leg dribble. His muscular shoulders leaned forward, but the ball missed his left hand and ended up in the hands of a Clinton guard, who raced down the court for a layup.

"He's giving them points," I murmured to Gaby on my right and Travis on my left.

"Get him out of there," Gaby responded.

"Tyree, get in for Latrell," I yelled.

I'd hoped the bench could give us direction. Instead it was more of the same nervousness and disoriented basketball. The corollary to missing a lot of practices is missing a lot of opportunities in a game. I had this feeling Latrell wasn't going to help us tonight. And it didn't make a difference if Tyree was playing well or not; he hadn't missed a practice, and at least he wasn't giving Clinton any buckets. My neck was in a death match with the starchy collar; the razor burn was starting another red trail around my neck.

Midway through the fourth quarter, we were actually down by only five points, 35–30. Down by five, on the road with a young team, so I thought, *Well, I hope this game helps us later on in the season and we can win a road game at Maspeth or Morrisania if we are ever down in the fourth.* I am convinced the only way to win a game down in the fourth quarter is to be madly in love with this sport. In the crowd I now spotted Caridad, Frankie's mom. At work she doesn't take lunch breaks so she can accumulate those hours and leave a little early to catch the games. Now, with his mom here, would Frankie deliver? He looked refreshed and confident. His confidence seemed to spread throughout the team. We looked more poised. A shot of confidence was what we needed. Every time a Clinton player drove into the paint, Charles, who has a peculiar silent intensity, was there to block his shot. He was redirecting shots. Anytime a Governor got close to the basket, he was able to deflect it or change the direction of the shot. Coach Ballerini would later say, "Charles is one of the best shot-blockers I have ever coached against."

The blend of Charles's intimidating defense and a few timely baskets by Walfri and Frankie helped us finally take the lead. With two minutes remaining in the game, Walfri, brimming with confidence, grabbed a rebound and gained momentum with each dribble down the court. He scampered like an overfed bear. At this point in the game, we want to remove some seconds from the clock before we shoot, but Walfri had another plan. He dribbled into a wall of defenders and lost the ball out of bounds.

Walfri thought he was fouled and was about to pursue the referee, when Charles and Tyree headlocked and bear-hugged him, respectively. If they hadn't grabbed Walfri, he might have received a technical foul and changed the course of the game.

We were up 43–35 with about thirty-five seconds left.

Clinton missed. There was a lot of holding and grabbing. This time Charles got the ball and was fouled immediately. He missed the front end of the one-and-one. We were not going to escape this game (or this season) if we didn't hit our free throws.

Without hesitating, the tall, lanky Clinton guard grabbed the rebound and dribbled up the court and calmly hit a fifteen-footer. Time-out Clinton. Up 43–37, I decided it was time to throw a touchdown pass. I have this favorite out-of-bounds play where we throw the ball the length of the court; it usually gets us a layup every three years. This time the ball was intercepted. Someone should have grabbed me before I decided on that play. Too much coaching. Sometimes we poke holes in our own life preservers.

Twenty seconds had elapsed, and the score remained 43–37, I hoped.

I checked with Travis. "What's the score?"

"Forty-three to thirty-seven," he said reassuringly.

Clinton ball. Number 13, the fearless guard who hit the fifteen-footer on the last possession, dribbled smoothly down the court. This time Frankie, our best defender, was in front of him. Tyree converged on him from behind his ropy arm and waited to swat the ball from another ropy arm. With eight seconds on the clock, all three collided around twenty feet from the rim, and somehow the shot went in: 43–40 with the foul. Frankie opened his mouth in disbelief as the court was suddenly filled with disbelieving students from the stands; I saw an emerald-green winter jacket, a pink vest, a young lady in tight blue jeans, a periwinkle hoodie all storm the court. The court looked like a bowl of Fruity Pebbles.

Walfri put his arm around Tyree in a gesture that resembled a big brother letting the little brother know he messed up.

The Clinton coaching staff helped remove the fans from the court. Once everyone was settled back into the stands, the younger ref, after conferring with Napolitano, made the T sign with his hand: a technical foul for crowd-control issues. Well, not all refs are created equal. Nonetheless, the Clinton assistant coach was about to lose his head.

Walfri looked at me and gave the flick-of-the-wrist motion indicating that he would shoot the technicals. I point my finger at Frankie. I am forever choosing sophomores over seniors. Frankie calmly made both free throws. Number 13 missed his free throw. "Forty-five to forty." Travis conveyed the good news, like a warm samovar used to greet me on cold winter nights in Moldova.

Our ball. Quick foul. Frankie again made both free throws. As the buzzer sounded, Walfri and Tyree skipped like bighorn sheep across half-court into the celebratory scrum. We had outscored Clinton 25–13 in the fourth quarter to escape the grand Basketball Palace of Knossos with a 47–40 victory. Frankie had 20 points, 5 assists, 7 rebounds, 4 steals, 1 block, and only 1 turnover in the second half. Charles had 9 points, 12 rebounds, and 8 blocks: almost a triple-double. We returned to our makeshift locker room. Undefeated.

"It's obvious we need more practice."

Tyree, Walfri, and I had all tried a little hero ball tonight, and it failed. Lesson learned. Clearly we are not ready to harpoon any whale, or even a goldfish. But at least we got a Governor tonight. Win number one on the season was also win number two hundred for my career.

"That was number two hundred," I whispered to Gaby on our way down the stairs. Gaby was a player when I won my first game against South Bronx Prep in the winter of 2006.

"Congratulations."

As we got outside we shared a quick embrace and he walked the team to the train. The moon hung brightly in the chilly November night sky. To a coach, his team is much more than an after-school activity. Last season, after a loss at Gompers High School, I stood in the cold dark February night feeling worthless, alone, and hungry, staring at the infinite darkness of our skies waiting for a cab. Tonight, the cab could take its time. I was going to enjoy this win.

I get home and my after-game ritual starts: wash the jerseys, enter the stats, upload the game film, eat dinner, read bedtime stories, catch up with Jessica, and go to bed. I lay in bed awake for hours; the residual adrenaline of tonight's win wouldn't let go. I got up and walked to the kitchen. I checked my phone and saw a few text messages from Latrell sent at two a.m.

"No more lies I wanna tell you the truth. I've lied a lot over the years because I wasn't as committed as I should've been. I just don't really like school. I hate going, but I do love basketball and the only way to play that and actually try and pursue that is to go to school. I learned that the hard way. I'm really sorry Coach."

For over two years Latrell had done his best to rescue himself each time he self-defenestrated with some elaborate excuse. I remembered wondering if Latrell would make it through this season. Would I have to throw him off? I started scrolling through the timeline of texts from Latrell: Babysitting, grounded. Lies, lies.

Latrell's conundrum was solved the next day with his final salvo via text:

"Coach? I didn't know how to say this before but . . . I quit the team. It's doing too much to my legs. I don't know what's wrong with them yet, but it's been going on for a while. I can't tolerate the pain anymore and I've tried in practice but it just made me look really slow and it hurt too much to push myself. Sorry Coach it was great playing for you. Best Coach anyone could ask for."

He would quit by telling everyone he had a painful knee injury and was done for the season. It might even have been true. I was never the wiser to any other reasons he must have quit.

I couldn't really celebrate my two hundredth career victory the way I wanted because it was sandwiched between two forwards quitting the team and a longtime assistant coach saying good-bye.

The next morning, I was physically sore.

A friendly dad at Nina's bus stop asked, "Did you guys win last night?"

"Yes, by seven."

Another dad asked, "Who did you play?"

"DeWitt Clinton."

"That makes the Clintons 0-2 this November."

I had been an eyewitness to a gritty win, which usually feels pretty good. But there was a pinch in my heart trying to figure out why Latrell and Brandon had defected from the team. I thought back to the guys celebrating. That's the feeling we chase as coaches. But there is another feeling of pain that is unsettling.

When I got home from work, Nina had drawn a basketball fairy and decorated it with two hundred stars that spelled "Congrats Papa." We opened up league play on the Monday after Thanksgiving. We had a week without a game. I wondered if anyone else would quit.

OUR SCHOOL

Imagine yourself at a prestigious New Hampshire high school in the spring of 1993. The bucolic campus is in bloom, college acceptance letters are in, and dreams about the future are palpable. The timing is perfect, the senior class is on the cusp of transforming themselves into something new. There are more than two thousand students here, but you feel at home here because it's a place where everyone knows your name. This type of atmosphere breeds confidence, hope, and magnanimity.

Now place yourself in a public high school of similar size in the Bronx at the same time. The campus is walled with iron gates and patchy grass, and since most of your friends are not graduating—in fact only about 12 percent of the student body graduates from here—nobody is really thinking about the future. Here you are anonymous. You spend hours in the hallways and most adults ignore you. You cling to your friends because if you're seen alone you might get jumped. This type of atmosphere breeds confusion, despair, and bitterness.

In the early 1990s, it became impossible to continue to ignore the failures of the New York City public school system. Perusing the graduation rates, one becomes horrified. Thirty percent. Twenty-two percent. Twelve percent! Desperation forced the city to act. In 1993, Julia Richman High School in Manhattan was closed and was replaced by several smaller high schools. After the Julia Richman High School experiment, then–New York City Schools chancellor Ramon C. Cortines and a team of educators sought to close other large failing high schools throughout the city. He toured the city like a king tours his empire. In Queens, Brooklyn, and the Bronx he found the same scenario: large groups of students in the hallways, and small circles of students in classrooms with beleaguered teachers behind locked doors. One day while at Monroe High School in the Bronx, the chancellor was attacked by an angry young student.

When I first heard this story, I immediately thought of the spasmodic teenager Gavrilo Princip, the Bosnian Serb who in 1914 assassinated Archduke Franz Ferdinand of Austria and the archduke's wife, Sophie, while they visited disgruntled sections of their own empire. The assassination sparked World War I, ended the Habsburg Empire, and gave birth to nation-states throughout Europe. Similarly, the attack on the chancellor by a resentful teenager, while I bet not as coordinated as that fateful day in Sarajevo, had a similar effect on another failing institution, New York City public high schools. After the unfortunate if contingent incident, it was clear to Ramon Cortines what school needed to be rescued from the educational abyss.

You might want to ask, who were the tribunes who allowed

anger, hostility, discontent, and apathy to invade urban public education? That is not the right question to ask. School failure didn't happen on its own. It was the culminating result of decades of neglect, white flight, and poor political decisions. A better question is, how do you avoid anger, hostility, discontent, and apathy in a school? What happened in the early 1990s in New York City, to borrow a phrase from Gershom Scholem, can only be called history's "plastic hours." This is "when sentiments of hope spread across the globe." For a short time, a few people were able to wrestle the failing school template from the educational traditionalists: those who think that the only type of schooling that worked for them should work for everyone. The breakup of large, failing high schools paved the road for a new type of high school in America's largest city. Many influential people sharpened the blade that cut these failing schools apart, mainly the Coalition of Essential Schools and the Annenberg Foundation, followed by the Gates Foundation. They are responsible for the births of many more small schools, not just in the Bronx, but across the nation.

Where did the idea come from? Was it the offspring of Debbie Meier's smaller schools in East Harlem? Was this school the brainchild of the marriage of John Dewey and Horace Mann? Or was it an offspring of Theodore Sizer's notion that one type of school doesn't fit all students? Or was it the visionary New York State education commissioner Thomas Sobol's magnanimous gift that allowed these small schools to be exempt from the New York State Regents Exams?

In short, yes. They and many others were responsible for improving the lives of students and families across New York. Fannie Lou's founding principal, Peter Steinberg, and his pioneering teaching staff tried to answer the problem of educating America's poorest children by bringing forth a school that would know its students and know them well. It was not only an effort to upgrade education in the Bronx, long a spot for neglect, where violence was common and apathy contagious, but a resolve to treat students and their families well. In 1994, the staff at Fannie Lou opened up the doors to the same students who had attended Monroe High School, the second-most-violent school in the city, and changed lives simply by knowing and caring who these children were.

In the early 2000s, the Bloomberg administration was bullish on expanding the small schools movement. More than two hundred small schools have been created in New York. Many of the same people involved helped build other small schools that did not succeed. Schools are incapable of divorcing themselves from politics. But since some new small schools were unable to rid themselves from their traditional education leanings, they became schizophrenic: small progressive schools in form, but traditional in content. Some of the new smaller schools were thinly disguised as progressive schools. They were set up the same way they always had been and were unable to transcend the bell versus the curriculum (the schedule against what should be taught), the lecture versus discovery, the hands-on experiments versus textbooks.

Recently, many small schools have been forced to merge with other small schools. I have asked myself many times, how does a school not fold unto itself? Ralph Waldo Emerson said, "An institution is the lengthened shadow of one man." Well, Mr. Emerson, the shadow of one woman is responsible for Fannie Lou's continued success. It is without question Nancy Mann, a founding teacher and the principal of Fannie Lou Hamer Freedom High School from 2002 to 2014 who actualized and established the school, its curriculum, and its schedule, and who inspired the students. It is also fair to say she raised a lot of teachers, myself included. Nancy Mann is a substitute matriarch for me and many other educators who now themselves operate small schools throughout the city. Like many of my veteran colleagues, we were single when we started working there. We soon married. And now many of us have children, and our children play with one another. Nancy fostered a school where teachers learned how to become teachers, students were no longer anonymous, and families in the Bronx now had an excellent place to send their children to be educated.

In 1994, as you can imagine, Fannie Lou had some of the most difficult students in New York City. Some of the teenagers, because of educational neglect and interruptions in their schooling, read at a second-grade level. To build a school and for that school to remain successful, certain structures needed to be built. Students would have block scheduling: two-hour classes instead of the traditional forty-two minutes. The school day was streamlined. Math and science, once jealous cousins, would now be dressed alike and taught together, by the same teacher. Literature and history, competing brothers, would now have to share a bunk and be taught by the same teacher.

Each teacher had an advisory. "Advisory" is a modern take on the vintage homeroom. The advisory classroom is infused with a guarantee that every student in the school will have a teacher who will advocate for them. Someone who knows them well enough to write a glowing college recommendation, triage minor incidents before they become full-blown emergencies, add a different adult voice in their young lives that is nonacademic, offer advice about life or school, or just be someone to talk to. The quotidian dynamics of shuffling all over the building between classes are eliminated. On the top floor, the eleventh graders loop for two years with the same teachers. On the first floor, the ninth and tenth graders stay with the same teachers for two years. Teachers teach a two-year cycle—an arrangement called "mixed-age classrooms." Students are designated to two or four classrooms, which are referred to as a "house" or "division." The school was built so caring teachers would know students well. I need to underscore that the two-hour classes and the advisory with the same teachers for two years are designed so that students would spend time with adults and other students whom they grow to trust. Therefore teachers can help children who live on the margins of society build the skills they need to succeed and change their lives.

There is a charm to the building on 1021 Jennings Street. Picture this: When you walk in, you can hear candidates for student government giving stump speeches in the cafeteria. Walk down the hall. Here you will see Marilyn Byrd's literature classroom, which traces its origins to a tasteful literary parlor. I like to think this is what an independent bookstore would do if space and overhead weren't an issue. The walls are a canary blue. There are lamps scattered across the room. The windows have white curtains that breathe rhythmically throughout class, where whispering teenagers, tucked with their books, silently read to themselves. A haunting red and white handmaid's dress hangs from the ceiling, adding a chilling dystopian accent to the calmness she has otherwise created in her room.

Move from the serenity of Marilyn's room to the game show atmosphere of Chloe Prieto and Monique Dozier's math class. Symmetry abounds. The room is decorated colorfully with student work. Teenagers raise anxious hands hoping to guess the right answers. The math here is serious, yet Chloe and Monique manage to maintain a sense of humor, like a constant function in an algebra problem. There is the perfect amount of levity and numeracy all in one room. In one particularly remarkable example, Chloe sent a struggling student numerous emails and stayed after school multiple days to help him create his own isometric puzzles and prove his own geometric ideas. Overall, students are deeply engaged with the work they are creating, but even the ones who don't want to work, those who are obstinate and resistant, are going to get harassed, for lack of a better word, by a teacher's persistence.

It's a short walk from math to physics. In Andy Brosoff's room, students are designing their own roller coasters. They are busy experimenting, predicting, and calibrating the potential and kinetic energy of their own flying death machines. This type of engagement spares the students the boring, tedious, and formulaic approach to physics, where they are responsible for finding answers to someone else's problems. Here they have to solve their own problems, for their own ride. Andy is there to remind them about momentum and acceleration, to pay attention to the strict gravitational rules that govern our planet. Andy moves across the room with a propulsive force combined with sheer middle-aged seriousness. The students trust his sincerity, and Andy encourages them to make mistakes. Again, you always see students working, teachers coaching.

Near Andy's room is my room. Here we are going to pause for a moment and try to devour history. Before I can convince any student to eat some historical ideas, I need to do some preparation. Some philosophies will need to be defrosted. Others microwaved. Others have expired and need to be discarded.

The teachers know the emphasis of the school is on the child. The student is the worker; the teacher is the coach. At the same time, if the school is communal, then teaching in the classrooms is wholly individual. A school like Fannie Lou can be looked at as a house with different rooms. The commonality of Marilyn's reading room, Chloe and Monique's mathematical game room, and Andy's garage kids tinkering and making things. My room is a pragmatic kitchen. All share in the essence of an education at Fannie Lou.

Admittedly, progressive education has its challenges. The advocates for a traditional model and test preparation have a point. There are certainly poems to decipher, mathematical rules to memorize, and historical dates that children need to know. The only problem is, which poems, what mathematical rules, and which dates are mandatory? Let the argument commence.

High-stakes testing may help prepare children for the other exams in their lives. There will be entrance exams for college and certification tests for future employment. There's a sense that early-in-life exams groom students to be practiced test-takers and therefore become successful adults. But if children are passively spending hours upon hours silently rehearsing for an exam, they are also spending hours upon hours not dancing, not drawing, and more importantly not playing, debating, or discussing. I have to ask, when are they thinking creatively?

With traditional education and high-stakes exams, there is an imposition of middle-class values and an erroneous assumption about what education really is. Progressive education teaches us that memorization doesn't sprint alongside knowledge. It succeeds only in resembling true understanding. There's a pitfall in standardization. It ruins the individual. I enjoy the other side of the educational coin, the side where the beauty is in the discovery of something new.

Progressive education embraces the individual. All schools need multifaceted teachers who care. At Fannie Lou, there are two dozen classrooms operating with students who are driving longer and diving deeper into topics. We have the ingredients for a solid education. A large industrial-size high school, in contrast, is fertile ground for kids to be anonymous, for teachers to burn out, and for apathy to spread among both. Small schools graduate more students. Small schools are safer. Small schools have changed the city that we know. Some experts are now linking New York City's decrease in homicides to the increase in small schools. More kids feel like they have a school where someone cares about them. In large high schools, you have no idea what people are doing during those crucial years. I went to a large high school, but it wasn't until college, when I wasn't a popular athlete anymore, that I experienced academic anomie. The anonymity of a small school will last mere hours, after which there are plenty of adults and kids who will know your name. A large high school, on the other hand, can create a lifetime of hostility toward schooling and teachers. In a small school, students have a school that knows them well. They have agency and are actors in their own lives. I think of schools as an engine that helps this city operate. Small schools save lives.

There's no questioning the brilliance and durability of the formula of Fannie Lou. Marilyn joined the staff in 2008. Andy has been here since 2011. Our classrooms reflect ideals that are basic to the foundations of public education: equity, democracy, and engagement. The faculty works together. We are friends.

The way the school is structured, I know exactly what the 2017 Panthers are working on every day. Today Frankie practiced his lines for his *Macbeth* performance. Tyree and Kaleb went to the Bronx River to measure its turbidity and salinity. Walfri wrote a paper on Emmett Till. Charles wrote the second chapter of his autobiography. Shamar presented his PowerPoint on "parenting and inequality." Cris worked on his microbes mini-lab. Kenneth and Mack compared political cartoons about the Cuban Missile Crisis. Josh and JB worked with their advisers on the differences between private and public colleges. Bryant edited a draft on the idea of greed in Pushkin's *Queen of Spades*. The members of the basketball team all have the common spirit of the school.

Over the years, I have worked hard to sharpen my sales pitch. Fannie Lou was built to provide a quality education and lure families from the neighborhood. Its magnetism has worked on me and my colleagues as well. As anyone who has ever taught in an urban public school knows, teaching is no joke. It is a very difficult job. You do have to be a badass once in a while. I'm fortunate to work here, though. Gone are the clunky, impersonal forty-minute periods, gone are the overpopulated schedules where teachers interact with hundreds of students a day. As teachers, we are unencumbered by conventional thinking. As a result, a dozen or so colleagues have embraced Fannie Lou for the long haul. They aren't distracted by changing jobs or careers. They have given themselves a chance to grow their roots here.

When I check my colleagues' social media, it is not uncommon to see the love they have for Fannie Lou. One morning I saw Kate Belin post a photo on Instagram. It was of her shadow on the wall of the school with a leafless tree behind her. She used the hashtag "roots."

Fannie Lou has a centripetal pull. Ask anyone who has ever worked there. This is not to say that those who left did not love it. How does Fannie Lou keep up the high standards and ideals? A combination of allegiance, faith in the institutional organization, and a little luck.

In 1993, the chancellor was attacked by a young man who was discontented, not because he was left alone in the hallways, but because he was allowed to be anonymous. Teaching at Fannie Lou is not like any movie you've ever seen about teaching. Maybe it is more like the old television show *Cheers,* because here at Fannie Lou, everyone knows your name.

HOME OPENER

In our home opener we looked royally good in our inglorious, unluxurious gym. And the good news was that over the last few days, nobody had quit the team. Tony, Randy, and Steven, the school custodians, kept it *makpid* as a kosher restaurant. We beat Annex High School 75–47. The first quarter was redolent of the first game against Clinton, but after that we blew them out of the gym. In our next home game of the season, we had what I will call a Julius Caesar game. We "wreaked havoc and unleashed the dogs of war" on Hyde Charter School, 105–53. Sometimes I have to be indecorous on the sideline to get the team to play the way I want. Tonight was one of those nights. Clearly the only thing I can accomplish against the rapid growth of charter schools is to beat their teams. That's my digital salute to the charter schools movement. We were now 3-0 on the season. Up next was our division rival, Morrisania.

THE ALBATROSS

After school on game days, my classroom transforms into the locker room for the basketball team. Sneakers, jeans, belts, socks, duffel bags, and T-shirts today cover Emilio Aguinaldo's Independence Day Speech; there are still copies from yesterday's lesson on Teddy Roosevelt's "The Man in the Arena" on the table. My room is a mess. The old diagrams from previous seasons, along with clinic notes and motivational articles that were never read or are now forgotten, surround a favorite article from *Grantland* on top of a file cabinet. A green scorebook from 2010 sits alone on the windowsill; the basketball ephemera compete with the daily assignments and forgotten papers with the signatures of students who either forgot to take them, didn't think it was necessary, or figured I would keep them in a safe place. I bet on the latter and put the papers on the enormous, space-invading computer cart. Three Band-Aid-colored file cabinets squat in the back of my room stuffed with clothes, shoes, yearbooks, and more papers. Paper is the ultimate colonizer. Its imperial expansion is difficult for me to keep up with and still keep a tidy classroom. By 3:30 p.m., the guys were dressed and the routine of the pregame chalk-and-talk was about to begin.

"Frankie, can you get your shoes off the table, it's bad luck."

Frankie removed a pair of pearl-white Jordans and placed them on the floor politely.

The role superstitions play in a season can be crippling. I haven't shaved since the day before the Clinton game. There are strings of gray hair on my chin that weren't there last year. My beard has traces of cinnamon too; it reminds me of a pancake with powdered sugar sprinkled on top. You would think the older I get, the less superstitious I would become. Not so. I'm reminded that Nikita Khrushchev tried to implement a fight against superstitions. He also wanted people to eat more corn. I'm not convinced I would have been a good Soviet citizen.

Last season Morrisania finished second in our division. They were a tough-minded opponent, and many of the players on both teams had been playing against each other since middle school.

"Take care of the ball, be aggressive on defense, and play together."

Those were my simple suggestions for the early December divisional game. We were still turning the ball over at an alarming rate, and it was freaking me out. Turnovers are hard to solve.

"Ready? Let's go!"

We huddled in the front of the room near the chalkboard, and Walfri led us with a "One, two, three, defense, four, five, six, together!" chant.

Checklist: camera, tripod, clipboards, dry-erase markers, red defibrillator, and the scorebook were all picked up as the boys shuffled out of the room to the gym. I felt like we were missing something. Jaquan, the junior backup point guard, wasn't with us today. He had to babysit or was grounded or was grounded for not babysitting. I wasn't really sure. At that moment, I remembered his mom had texted me earlier in the day asking me to send him home right after school. I forgot to tell the team.

In the gym, some popular hip-hop music played. The students in the crowd were mouthing the lyrics. Tyree was flashing his hands and enjoying the songs. I'm never sure what song or artist is playing. I don't care what music they listen to as long as it helps them. Tyree, the fifteen-year-old shooting guard, looked like a consummate ventriloquist while effortlessly making the ball go through the hoop. He and Shamar had just created the "Shooting God" T-shirt, pinching the Houston Rockets' Chris Paul's "Point God" moniker. Ty loved to shoot. He was driven by a mimetic compulsion like a machine. He frequently changed his last name on social media to Ty Briscoe or Ty Fox or Ty Oubre, borrowing the surnames of talented college or NBA players. I could see the scars on his right forearm; the sun had darkened the scar on the top, leaving the two on the underside a flesh color. His left shoulder was now pinned with a tattoo saying "Faith." Melville wrote, "Faith, like a jackal, feeds among the tombs, and even from these dead doubts she gathers her most vital hope." I was hoping our shooting guard would start shooting the ball well.

Tyree's basketball off-season hadn't gone exactly as planned. The injury prevented him from playing for the rest of the summer. His new bionic arm was a little rusty. He struggled in the preseason, but in the last couple of practices and games he had looked more comfortable. "Just keep shooting," I told him during practice. Later that night he sent a text: "Life throws challenges at you, you need to face them." Ty was well aware of his struggles. He was staying late after practice and shooting in the morning before school started. Nonetheless, he was shooting under 10 percent on three-pointers. Yet today in warm-ups he looked like Ray Allen: the ball wasn't even hitting the rim. All net.

The Morrisania coach, Steven Greenwald, is a retired teacher, but he still coaches basketball to stay active during retirement.

He was wearing a blue New York Yankees polo shirt and khaki cargo shorts with black ankle socks, as if summer hadn't vanished months ago. I stood as far away from him as possible, yet he approached me. There is something suspicious about a coach who arrives at a game dressed like a vendor at a baseball game. The pregame coaching exchange is as painful as you can imagine. He wouldn't stop speaking in baseball metonyms and retirement mumbo jumbo and lamenting about teenagers and their lack of work ethic. "Wheelhouse." "Tier four versus tier one." You get the picture.

Ms. Jackson was waving at me from across the gym. She was rescuing me from this ordeal.

"Best of luck tonight," I squeezed out of the corner of my lips to my garrulous opponent and skimmed across the court to her.

The game was about to start, when Gaby leaned over. "Oh, I see this guy at the Laundromat all the time."

"Who?"

"The ref. He's awful. He watches games the same way I stare at clothes in the dryer."

Charles reappeared just in time from the storage room, which serves as a Seamen's Bethel before games; he prays alone before each game there. Charles tapped the tip perfectly to Frankie. Frankie snatched the ball, the Morrisania defenders moved like starfish, and Frankie quickly took two dribbles and soared above them for an easy bucket. He hovered and turned in the air to get back on defense. For a moment he looked like a helicopter in a premature landing.

Frankie's basket would be our best offensive possession of the first half and his last bucket of the game. Nobody heard the crack, a few saw the grimace, and only Frankie felt the microfissure in his foot. I was waiting for the injury to subside; like stepping on an errant Lego, the sting eventually fades. He hobbled back on defense dutifully, lifting his right foot in the air. The clock operator was looking at Frankie. The guys on the bench were looking at Frankie. Gaby stood up. The whole time I was trying not to look at Frankie.

I finally found someone to rest my eyes on, in the stands: Jamaal Lampkin, class of 2010. Jamaal now looked like a full-back, but when he played for me he was a relentless rebounder and the first 1,000-point scorer in the history of Fannie Lou. Our eyes met as Frankie hobbled in front of us the way someone walks in front of the television.

Watching Frankie limp was unsettling. We had seen this sort of injury before and knew it wasn't good. Was it his Achilles? His ankle? I didn't know. Frankie just seemed to land the wrong way.

Gaby and Frankie disappeared into the weight room. I hesitated. Coaches are never supposed to hesitate. Mack was home babysitting. So now, early in the season, we didn't have a third-string point guard. Now I would have to apply the sacred principle of injuries: the next guy better be ready.

"JB, get in there."

Tyree and Shamar, like bear cubs separated from their brother, were looking in the direction of the weight room, hoping Frankie would reemerge from the hobble. "Shamar, you are now the one," I said, shifting the burden of point guard duties onto him. He told me later that when he heard me say that, he said to himself, "IQ now needs to go up and nerves need to go down."

The Morrisania Knights were energized by Frankie's disappearance and scored easily on the next possession. They applied a full-court press, since they knew that without our regular point guard we would have difficulty. Walfri, our dependable inbounder, passed to Shamar, who was clearly not ready to take over the point guard duties, because he found the person with the least amount of experience against a full-court press, the freshman Jaelen, "JB." I imagine he was a very good eighth-grade player. He's athletic and strong, but at five-ten, he was now far from the tallest or strongest on the court. Unbridled like a bottle rocket, he quickly dribbled up the right sideline. His flame was quickly extinguished by three Morrisania defenders. JB's shot still managed to ricochet off the backboard the way a carpenter bee slams against a window in vain. The rest of the quarter was a lot more of JB's unspectacular fireworks, forcing shots into a defensive hurricane of Morrisania arms and hands.

"Is he ready?" I asked Gaby.

Gaby went to check on Frankie.

"No. He says it hurts on the top of his foot."

A few more possessions went by.

"Is he ready?"

"He says he is in a lot of pain."

"He may have broken something," I admitted. Frankie was not a malingerer.

On the defensive end, we fouled them on every other possession. Jaelen launched another unmakable shot, and finally I had to take him out of the game.

Yet somehow we were winning 13–11 at the end of the first quarter.

"Jaelen, we play as a team. You're not going to beat them yourself. Relax out there and let the game come to you. You're forcing everything, you don't have to score to help us. In fact, don't try to score."

I don't think he heard me.

"Bryant, go in for JB, tell Charles he is the four [power forward], and Walfri is the three [the small forward]."

Bryant, the backup center, now entered the game. His Bajan Rastafarian braids covered his eyes like those decorative bead curtains from a long-lost college dorm room. He may or may not have given the directions I asked.

To start the second quarter, Shamar was now at point guard

for the first time in his life. Ty was ice-cold from the outside. Walfri was now at the small forward spot, a position he has dreamed of playing, but his Clydesdale speed had always prevented it. Only Charles and Bryant were at positions they knew well.

What happened next was unpleasant. I would call a play, and nobody knew where they were supposed to be.

"T-Stack," Shamar called, trying to redirect the troops. It was our pet play, where Walfri usually gets a layup.

Shamar veered. Tyree tacked. Nobody was in the position. The play plunged into oblivion.

Frankie had reappeared and taken up two chairs on the westernmost part of the bench. A gap of three chairs developed between him and four players with about ten minutes of varsity experience combined—Kenneth, Kaleb, Cris, and Jaelen. On nights like tonight, we could have used Xavier and Latrell. I wanted to text Mack, "Next time listen to your mom, please." The best-laid plans can be undone by an injury, a lie, or a punishment. Walfri moved to correct the situation and caught the ball, but he traveled as he tried to attack the paint. A few plays later, a combination of a Shamar steal and layup allowed us to apply our full-court pressure. Guys were *almost* in their right positions and were *almost* getting steals. They looked like teenagers driving a car for the first time.

The gym was silent until Bryant got a block that awoke his four friends in the stands. A small fan club attended every game, waiting for any little thing that Bryant did right so they could lose their minds. Next was Tyree's turn. He snagged a pass and went in for a layup. Tyree then went on to have back-to-back-to-back steals and was able to find Shamar sprinting ahead for an easy bucket. Our defense was keeping us alive.

Unaccustomed to playing a lot of minutes, Bryant asked for a rest. Did the bench time teach JB anything? Maybe. As soon

as he touched the ball, he drove right into the paint and found
Tyree for a wide-open three. That may have been our second-
best offensive possession of the game.

"Great pass, JB!" Frankie yelled.

We would fight back before halftime to be down only five:
28–23.

"Is Frankie okay?" Frankie's cousin asked.

"I think it's best if he went to the hospital now." We asked his
cousin to take him there.

The third quarter proved to be a little better for us. However,
Tyree and Shamar were now taking turns throwing the ball
into the stands. "What are you doing?" an incredulous voice
from the crowd asked. I was uncharacteristically taciturn.
Usually, at this point I would have broken a clipboard, but since
I had already picked up a technical foul in the first quarter I
remained seated and calm. Thinking of Frankie with a broken
foot, I felt dazed and nauseated.

A Walfri three-pointer cut the lead to 34–31 with under four
minutes to play in the third quarter. Morrisania's 1–2–2 half-
court zone was still giving us problems. On the next play they
executed a textbook pick-and-roll.

"If they keep doing this, we are in trouble," I said to Gaby.

We were running out of answers. A lively chant of "Panthers,
Panthers, Panthers" arose from the otherwise-sober crowd.
"Run Special for Shamar," a baseline out-of-bounds play where
Shamar splashed a three-pointer, put us up 43–35. Shamar now
had more points in his first four games than he had all last
season. This was his second 20-point game this season. The
momentum wasn't enough. The pendulum swung back with a
few miscues, and we were up only three, 43–40, at the end of
the third.

To start the fourth quarter, the Morrisania point guard

swished a three-pointer to tie the game. Shamar deftly, and now more confidently, drove the lane and found Walfri for a layup. The intensity of the game increased.

"Get that shit out of here!" Charles yelled after a block.

Technical fouls, even though blown on the same black whistle, always sound a little different than regular ones. Harsh. Authoritarian.

Shamar peeled the ball away for another steal and layup. He reminded me tonight of Dennis Johnson, the great Celtics point guard who could pilfer the ball from an opponent almost at will. Walfri and Shamar ran a pick-and-pop that unfolded in slow motion. Shamar used the screen to pass to Walfri, who then was blitzed by two defenders. Charles knowingly flashed to the free-throw line, caught Walfri's pass, pivoted, and found Shamar open on the other side for a three-pointer. Up seven: 50–43. We were playing team basketball.

Tyree forced a Morrisania player left, and the ball squirted and squiggled and eventually strolled alone toward our basket. Tyree dove for the ball, but it eluded him like a squid on ice. He bounced off the ball onto his back. Charles scooped up the slick, sweaty ball at half-court and with two lightning-fast dribbles skywalked toward the rim. His sneakers were now at his defender's chin.

"Bang!" The sweet sound of a dunk in the fourth quarter.

Charles turned, stone-faced, always unimpressed with himself, and got back on defense.

This dunk put the crowd into a frenzy. Kenneth, Kaleb, Bryant, and Cris, the remaining members on the bench, did what all great teams do: they cheered for their mates on the floor. Remember, the bench becomes the window into a team's soul.

Dunks late in the game have a sort of finality to them—they can evaporate any hope the other team has of winning. It was 54–46 with two and a half minutes remaining. After another

Morrisania time-out, I heard the slam of a clipboard on the ground. *Clang*—the sound of a missed opportunity. Then play resumed and the whistle blew. "Foul on number thirty-four." Walfri.

"That's his fifth," Gaby said.

Walfri was disqualified. A dejected Walfri walked slowly to the end of the bench, where Frankie had sat earlier, and buried himself in towels. Those towels were rewards for hard work; not unlike in the Stakhanovite movement, coaches love rewarding kids with material objects in the hope that it will create even more hard work. Still, I hate to see *the sulk* on the bench. I know that inimical sulking on the bench destroys team spirit. It's a wet blanket even on the forty-point win, but in a close game it can be fatal. The pubescent kick of the folding chair is timeless; it's the product of the competitive emotion that drives us to be disappointed most of the time in our own performance.

With Walfri upset and Frankie on his way to the hospital, winning a championship was the furthest thing from my mind. We were having trouble just beating Morrisania. The game wasn't even over yet, but our season might be. A disgruntled, underperforming senior, Walfri ended the game with 5 points. He had only 2 points against Annex last week. He was not happy. The magnificent victory over Clinton had vanished. Now everyone was rudderless. Against Hyde, it was scorched-earth basketball. No apologies. But not tonight. Not this team. The tide of the young season was pushing us out to sea.

Walfri was in complete sulk mode on the bench. He could have been cheering for his teammates on the floor, but he chose to sit there like a defeated boxer. With under a minute remaining, Charles took the ball out of bounds (something Walfri usually did for us), and he and Bryant, the center and the forward, passed it back and forth until a Morrisania player caught on to their little game and tipped it loose. A couple of collisions occurred, and the somnolent referee ran over to inspect the damage. Three or four players now tugged for the right to hold the ball, like teenage ladybugs on their backs, rocking the ball back and forth. The whistle sound interrupted the joust between Bryant and a Knight. Foul on Morrisania.

The biggest Knight on the court slapped the floor with his right palm, disagreeing with the call. Again the familiar sound of the whistle. This time the technical was on Morrisania.

Amid the confusion, Tyree walked up to the free-throw stripe. The septuagenarian refs were unable to agree on who got fouled, so Tyree shot the four free throws to push the lead back up to seven. Ball game.

WERNER HERZOG GETS ME THROUGH

We won without Frankie that night the way restaurants can stay open even if the executive chef is sick. But what kind of restaurant are we going to run without the top chef the rest of this season? Before our pursuit of the championship could even get under way, we'd lost our captain, our point guard, the oracle.

During a basketball season there are always plenty of head-winds: suspensions, injuries, unhappy players. Frankie's injury, a small fracture in his right foot, was a tornado. He was going to be out for the rest of the season. Something similar happened to us in 2014 when our leading scorer, Kenny Bonaparte, tore his ACL. That year I had five seniors who could handle the loss of Kenny, statistically and mentally. Sports are great, but injuries suck. Losing Kenny was the biggest blow I had experienced as a coach, up until now. Surely this year's team, much younger, would be severely hobbled without Frankie.

I turned to an unlikely source for comfort: the German film auteur Werner Herzog. Herzog had made *Fitzcarraldo* in 1982. The movie is not one of his best, I think, but the documentary of the making of *Fitzcarraldo* has become one of my favorites. *Burden of Dreams* captures what happens when a man with a camera and an idea attempts to make a movie in the middle of the Amazon. Mick Jagger, set to play the title character's assistant, quits. It's a lesson on what do you do when your big star bails halfway through the movie. Herzog has said that the Fitzcarraldo story represents "the victory of the weightlessness of dreams over the heaviness of reality." There are some real questions: Why doesn't Herzog just quit filming when he realizes the actors are getting sick, or when a small war between indigenous tribes breaks out? At one point Herzog admits the jungle is winning, but in the end he makes the movie. Herzog inspires me. If he could make that movie, I can coach under any conditions. Herzog said, "The real achievement of the film is that I finished it—that I would not stop, that I would not be scared away."

How the hell am I and these kids going to haul this boat over an isthmus in December? Faith. Conviction. Confidence. Hope. I kept repeating these words like a liturgical chant. Herzog said he would have climbed down to hell and wrestled the film out of the claws of the devil. My bags were packed and I was ready to do anything to win this title, except my team just lost its ladder, the zipper of my bag was broken, and I couldn't find my MetroCard.

GAME THEORY

On a windswept Friday night in December 2006, Jamaal Lampkin, a freshman forward, my wife, Jessica, and I were crowded together in the emergency room at Lincoln Hospital. Green and silver garlands hung over the doorways. "Feliz Navidad" could be heard from a radio somewhere. Christmas was fast approaching, but nothing could raise our dampened spirits. Jamaal, still in his home uniform, lay on a stretcher. A white sheet covered his legs. We'd just witnessed our team get trounced by eighty points. We really couldn't talk about anything. It was well past dinner. I offered Jamaal a Snickers bar from the vending machine to break the silence.

"Yo, Coach, are you trying to kill me?"

Somehow it had slipped my mind that Jamaal was allergic to peanuts. I meant no harm. He was already in rough shape. Sometime in the second quarter, Jamaal had jumped for a ball and come down on someone's foot, rolling his ankle. A painful but common basketball injury. Jamaal couldn't get up. He had trouble putting weight on his foot. Tarif Brown, a senior forward, and I carried Jamaal off the court toward the bench.

"Are you good, kid?" Tarif asked.

"I want to go back in, Coach," Jamaal requested.

Filled with teenage bravado but still in a lot of pain, Jamaal kept asking me to go back in, fighting back the tide of despair that was approaching. Noah Adler, an Oregonian and my trusty assistant coach at the time, ran to the nurse's office and grabbed a few ice packs. Jamaal sat at the end of the bench. Was he grimacing from the coldness of the ice pack or from ankle pain or from the agony emanating from the scoreboard? I was unsure. Nonetheless, he still tried to cheer for his beleaguered teammates.

—

No amount of cheering or goodwill could have stopped the carnage. As the score ballooned, the impropriety on the bench was unleashed. The guys on my bench removed their shoes while the game was in progress, signaling that they, like Jamaal, were also done for the night. Our opponents continued to apply a full-court press with their starting five until the final buzzer. What did we do to deserve that kind of beating? It was the ultimate comeuppance for a rookie coach who had won his first game two nights ago. Both teams had thrown out the rules that should govern blowout basketball. Was I coaching from a different era? This was definitely not New Hampshire high school hoops. Did I have a sepia-toned vision of basketball propriety and gamesmanship? Our opponent had all the height and athleticism that we didn't have, but did they have to win by eighty points?

Even in my embryonic stage of coaching I felt bench behavior was not just inextricably linked to winning, but also to a higher ideal of class and professionalism. I told myself that I had a lot left to learn. If I could teach myself Russian in Moldova, I could teach myself to coach basketball in New York City. Nonetheless, I was brand-new to coaching. We were all new to this. We had a lot of work to do, both on the court and off. At that moment we needed to get Jamaal to a hospital.

After the game I called his mom and we agreed to meet at the hospital. Here I was, a rookie coach, and I couldn't have dreamed of a worse beginning. Tonight was my home coaching debut, and not only did we lose by almost triple digits, but a promising freshman needed to be rescued by an ambulance. My head was spinning. I probably would have offered Jamaal strychnine if it was available in the vending machine.

When I took the job, I never imagined there would be nights like this. I thought coaching high school basketball would be easy. I wasn't prepared to cultivate leadership, to have players be mindful and most importantly enjoy playing the game we both loved. I had no experience managing egos, assessing injuries, building mind-sets where we don't quit if things aren't going well. I couldn't lead them to a path of self-discovery when I had no idea who I was or what I was doing. I didn't understand it was all about the relationships I would someday form. I was overwhelmed. In fact, I was like the Grinch: my heart was "two sizes too small" to coach.

Two days earlier, I was a coaching genius who had taken a winless team and won the first game I ever coached. As I left the court and headed toward the locker room, I had paused. I could hear the guys celebrating. Suddenly, I felt tears choking me. Something new and pleasurable had stirred in me. Why was I crying? Was it hope for the future of the team? Pride? I did something. They did something. We did it together. We conquered some limitations that the universe had put on us. Sure, it was only a win, but it felt a lot more important.

"I like this winning thing. Let's try it again on Friday," I had yelled.

Two nights later we were overwhelmed. I was clearly not prepared for what happened. I let my team get eaten by wolves. An impious coach just kept running up the score. The loss paralyzed our self-esteem. What happened that night was something that would never happen again. I was never going to get beat by eighty points again.

Sorrow, I discovered, doesn't let go of you after a loss. It sticks around like arthritis. When I found out Jamaal had broken his ankle, sorrow returned. Before his high school basketball career could even set sail, he was crippled with a serious leg injury. Jamaal wanted someday to play professional basketball. Now he thought his career was over before it even began. Injured chasing a dream; an Ahabian injury.

"Do you think I'll ever play again, Coach?" Jamaal asked.

"You will," I said.

There is a fundamental doubleness to the game: joy and pain. Jamaal and I were not able to take in these contradictions; the injuries and the losses were not what we wanted. To see the game in its entirety is what all coaches and players must learn to do. A rookie coach and a freshman were not ready to see that totality of the game.

I thought I knew just what to do after the loss: I made the next couple of practices unbearable. In fact, after every loss that season we ran and ran until they couldn't run anymore. They needed more discipline, I thought. Punishment for losing would make us a better team. I was uncompromising my first season. I wouldn't wash their practice uniforms until we won.

There are many paths to becoming a coach. In my fourth year of teaching at Fannie Lou, the fall of 2006, the former coach had stepped down and I became the head coach. I was a onetime bike messenger, a failed lab tech, a former Peace Corps volunteer who was looking to move abroad again. I had no business coaching a high school basketball team in New York City. I didn't want to invent myself again. I had left the sporting life behind me. It had served its purpose. I hung up the varsity jacket in 1993 after high school. Now, thirteen years later, I was back on the bench wearing a shirt and tie. Life is strange. Coaching was something I had never thought about before. Nor was it something I thought I would be doing for a long time. I was wrong.

After months of anticipation, we opened up the season in October 2006. I was struck by what the guys couldn't do on the court and ignored what they could do. Knowingly, they shot and dribbled with their palms. The game of basketball is performed on the fingertips for maximum control of the ball. Their footwork, essential in a game where once you stop dribbling your only move is to pretend one leg is glued to the floor and the other leg is free, was careless. I was a twenty-nine-year-old whose only qualification for coaching was that I played high school basketball in suburban New Hampshire.

Our first season, as you can imagine, was difficult. I inherited a winless team, clearly the worst team in New York City, where expectations were about as low as possible. But we would go on to win thirteen games and even make the playoffs. I still question my performance that year. Did I push my players too hard? Was I too demanding? Maybe. But later in the season, when we played the same opponent who had beat us by eighty, we lost by only nine! We won eighteen games my second year. The simple fact is that in my eleven years of coaching, we have never lost by eighty points again or anywhere close to it. You can't quibble with the results. We were winning.

After all these years, I still ask myself why I started coaching. Why would anyone get involved in it? At first you and your players will be stuck in the mire of overwhelmingness: overwhelming speed of the game. Overwhelming size of your opponent. Overwhelming attention to detail. Overwhelming number of offensive plays. Overwhelming number of hours committed to basketball. Overwhelming number of hours looking at film. Overwhelming number of days lifting weights, dribbling, shooting, hollering, pleading. Your players will be overwhelmed by the attention of girls, the media, the teachers, and eventually the attention becomes too much.

That night in December 2006, I was overwhelmed as I absentmindedly tried to hand the Snickers bar to Jamaal in the emergency room. I knew I had to prepare my team better. I grew into manhood with my first team. I squeezed every idea I could into the experience. At the end of the season I was sapped, hamstrung, saddled with an undisciplined style of basketball and a lovable team who were starved for positive attention. They returned the next year with renewed devotion, and that team would win a playoff game. I felt like we were building something special.

Four years later, Tarif Brown, the senior on the 2006 team, came back from college to visit me. We spoke about college, life outside the Bronx, what it felt like to come back.

"You know, Coach," Tarif said, "I would have never graduated high school without basketball."

Speaking with Tarif made me realize that coaching was a longitudinal enterprise.

Fortuitously, Tarif and I bumped into Jamaal in the hallway. He was now a senior, his ankle fully healed. He had had a fantastic basketball career, becoming Fannie Lou's first 1,000-point scorer. In his senior year we were 25-5; we'd come a long way. But toward the end of his senior year, Jamaal was still unsure what to do after high school. I left Tarif to talk to Jamaal, give him some advice. It was then that I felt like the Grinch again. You know the part, near the end of the story—where his heart grows three sizes bigger. I felt my heart grow warm. When I started coaching, I never imagined there would be days like this.

Jamaal Lampkin, even with a scar the size of a large hermit crab on his ankle, readily admits basketball saved his life. Tarif Brown lived with his brother his senior year and says that if it wasn't for the team, he might not have graduated and gone to college. In 2017, Tarif was training to become a principal and Jamaal is an IT specialist for Barclays. Winning is its own sweet reward, but Tarif and Jamaal showed me that the rewards they reaped later in their lives are tremendous and incalculable and reach far beyond basketball.

PRINCE DON'T MISS

Werner Herzog was able to finish his film because of a close friend, the actor Klaus Kinski, who played the role of Fitzcarraldo when Mick Jagger bailed. (Even though Kinski did threaten to kill him.) Charles was my Klaus Kinski. He had the leading role in our 2016–17 film. But I was worried about Charles. He said he felt betrayed by Latrell. They were best friends. They attended the same middle school, decided to come to the same high school together, and now their bond was breaking over a girl or lies or an injury. Charles had had enough heartbreak.

Once, after practice, he shared a story with me: One day, just like any other morning, Charles woke up to the sound of oil popping in the pan. He could smell fried eggs. There would be hardo bread with butter, okra, and some fried sole from last night's dinner on the table. There also would be sugarless tea that Charles wanted to add sweetener to.

"Prince, you have a game today?" Gramma asked.

"Mmmmm." Charles shook his head yes with a mouthful of food.

"I don't know what that means, but use words when you talk to me."

"Yes, Gramma." Charles laughed, knowing that was going to be her response.

He quickly ate his breakfast; even at ten, he wanted to be on time. First he needed to call his teammate, his best friend, one of those best friends who when you're ten feel like your brother.

"Prince going now?" Gramma asked.

"Yes," Charles responded.

"I know you're good and there are more shots you'll have to take in life, not only basketball," Gramma advised.

"Yes, Gramma, I know," Charles said. Charles was almost out the door when he heard her say, "Prince don't miss."

On the way to his best friend's, also named Prince, Charles spotted the neighborhood kids who were always getting in trouble.

"They were always messing with the neighbor, this middle-aged white guy," Charles told me.

That day the neighborhood kids were throwing rocks onto the white guy's porch.

Charles didn't want to do delinquent stuff with those kids. He also didn't feel like getting a beating from his grandmother.

Prince was five-eleven and Charles was five-nine; at eleven and ten, respectively, they were quite tall for their age. After the basketball game, they went back to Prince's parents' house. They couldn't sleep. They had permission to stay out in the yard.

They saw that "the boys who do dumb stuff" were outside also. "Hey, come with us?" they said. "You two soft?"

Charles and Prince knew it was way too late and that if they left the yard, there would be consequences. They watched as the boys ran onto the white guy's yard and started to throw rocks. One rock shattered a window. The white guy ran out of the house and started chasing them. They scattered. Charles and Prince were laughing until four of the boys ran toward them. The man stopped running, pulled a gun, and fired.

"All I heard was *Boom, boom, boom!!*" Charles said. The sound ripped open the silence of the night.

"The whole block was silent, nothing but the stench of the devil and a smoking gun were left," Charles said.

Charles and Prince froze with fear.

Boom. The gun fired again.

"I saw an angel get his wings clipped that day," Charles recalled Prince had said.

Boom. Another shot. This one hit Charles.

Charles remembered lights and commotion. He was put into an ambulance, where he fell asleep. His friend Prince died on the way to the hospital.

Charles wrote about this incident for an English class assignment:

> I woke up from the worst nightmare. Nothing but dizzy headaches and a numb pain along the right side of my body. I take my shots for Prince, the ghost that haunts me to do better and he's my giant that I stand on. I took the time to become a good student. I put more time into becoming a great basketball player. I've been teaching kids to play basketball since I left middle school. I'm in a fight, not with hands, but with the mind. I am mentally tough. I felt empty inside and might never walk, and I had to play basketball for me because I still have Prince with me.

Charles worked for almost a year just trying to walk again. Finally, he managed to walk without the aid of crutches. As he wrote:

> I had to run not only in sports but in life. Martin Luther King has been one of my most inspiring leaders that I was infatuated with. He said, "If you can't fly then run, and if you can't run then walk, if you can't walk then crawl, but whatever you do you always have to keep moving forward."

He was moved by Dr. King's words. "I couldn't fly so I fought till I could run." Now Charles was dunking nightly. He was flying all over the city.

THE CASTAWAY

I spent five unremarkable years at Northeastern, where I made few acquaintances, studied too much, spent too much money on punk rock shows at the Middle East and movies at the Brattle. I graduated with a degree in biology, with one eye on medical school, the other on plane fares. I looked cross-eyed at my first job with a college degree: a lab tech at Harvard Medical School. It was 1999, and the United States was dropping bombs on Serbia and I kept injecting insects with the wrong DNA. I injected *Drosophila melanogaster,* the common fruit fly, the geneticists' Frankenstein with wings, with different DNA strands, hoping these traits would be expressed in the next generation. Fruit flies die and reproduce incredibly quickly. I hated looking at them under a microscope. To this day, after I buy bananas from the grocery store I put them under cold water and wipe them down with a paper towel to prevent fruit flies from entering my apartment. Everything about the laboratory was dissatisfying—the repetitiveness of the day, the vibration of the vortex mixer, the people I worked with, the dismal paycheck, the dry scientific language we spoke, the pipettes, and of course the flies.

It felt like I had failed adulthood before it even started. Where was the life a college degree promised me? I couldn't believe this was it. I couldn't keep up with the work. I wasn't mixing the solutions correctly. One-molar solutions quickly became dilutions that clogged up the lab. My calculations were wrong. The microinjections were unsuccessful. The DNA wandered as if in a daydream away from its intended target. I wasn't precise enough, nor did I care enough. The flies weren't expressing the phenotypes they needed. They were failing me.

The job was supposed to help me get a letter of recommendation for medical school. Instead I was fired after a few months. For the next few years I'd work random jobs and travel to random countries. Hiked in Guatemala, visited a dude who took care of penguins in Patagonia, worked on a kibbutz in Israel, pretended to be down and out in Paris like George Orwell, except I couldn't even find a café to let me wash dishes and spit in the soup. Finally, when I was twenty-seven, it was time for a serious adventure, a full-on transformation. I had never been to the former Soviet Union. My undergraduate education had left me feeling incomplete, and traveling patched those holes. My mind still wandered to the old stone bridges I'd seen in the former Yugoslavia. I wanted to run away. I did what anyone who was in debt, jobless, and filled with bravado would do: I enlisted in the Peace Corps. Basically, though, when I left Boston in the early summer of 2001 with an ambitious reading list, a yellow tent, and a notebook, I was running away again. I told people I was chasing the ghost of Alexander Pushkin. The Pushkin who was exiled to Moldova and fell in love with a Gypsy girl.

It was easy to leave Boston. I didn't have a girlfriend or a career or even a pet. Joining the Peace Corps felt mandatory. I would learn to speak Russian, like Pushkin—that was how I thought of it. I could postpone my student loans, erase the embarrassment of being fired, fix the overwhelming feeling that I had still just finished college and my life wasn't working out the way I planned. I would spend two years in Moldova and return to America and finally become a doctor—that was the plan. Operation Bessarabia.

On the flight to Moldova, I sat next to a very attractive young woman. She held a copy of *The Ugly American* on her lap. Full of chutzpah and a passport equally overflowing with stamps, I attempted to impress her with my past travels and the blueprint of my future. We talked for hours.

"Why did you join the Peace Corps?" she inquired.

"Three reasons. One, to learn Russian. Two, to improve my résumé for medical school. Three, to change the world."

"Oh, you want to become a doctor?"

"That's the plan."

"Doctors live difficult lives. They don't make good husbands or dads." I was losing her somewhere over the Carpathians.

"Or a teacher," I stumbled.

"Teachers make good husbands and dads. They have respectable hours, summers off," she said.

"I'm Marc. What's your name?"

"Jessica."

It was a good recovery. Until then I had never actually thought about being a teacher. Hmm. Once I got to Moldova I buried the thought.

When we landed in Moldova and were situated in our hotel, I was able to write a few things down in my journal. I wrote about flying on a Yak, a Russian-made plane, and the tasteless and colorless airplane food. My final note was "I think I met my future wife today."

I spent two remarkable years in the poorest country in Europe. Unintentionally, Moldova trained me to survive on a peasant's diet. And, unintentionally, how to drink like my mom. I guess I could have abstained from drinking in Moldova, but that would be like jumping into the pool with your jeans on. Sure you're wet and you're having fun, but you look like an ass.

I changed my three goals after a few months in the Peace Corps. I still wanted to learn Russian, I now began to write, and I still wanted to change the world. I've done all right in the first two; the third is something I am still tinkering with. And then, in 2006, I married that young woman who had been sitting next to me thirty thousand feet in the sky.

THE DEATH STAR

It's now mid-December and the Panthers are 8-0. Gaby and I check the PSAL website daily. We share text messages about different teams. But really we were watching one team and one team only: the Cougars from South Bronx Prep.

"They scored 120 points last night."

"Against whom?"

"Bronx Early College, 120–43."

"Damn." I had the same feeling when the Death Star blew up Alderaan.

"Let's go see them. They play tomorrow night."

"Then get some Ecuadorian food?"

"Ceviche de pescado?"

South Bronx Prep was not only destroying teams, they had developed their own scorched-planet policy, a particular strategy General Sherman or even Darth Vader would have been proud of. This was "shock and awe" basketball. The box scores were mind-blowing and unnerving. South Bronx Prep was clearly becoming my "bitterest foe." I was impressed, annoyed, and scared.

Gaby, twenty-six, the son of Ecuadorian immigrants, is a loyal and dependable assistant coach, as well as a former player, which makes him invaluable. He tells everyone on the team, "I know what it is like to have Marc as a coach. Believe me, you have it easy." He has been with me since day one. Ten years ago, I never would have guessed Gaby would become the man I trust the most with my team. He was a decent player. He was easygoing and coachable. And now he was developing into a dedicated coach and dad.

In the fall of 2012, Gaby started coaching at the Fannie Lou Hamer Middle School across the street. At first glance I looked at it as just an after-school program. But Gaby kept asking me for drills and diagrams. I wasn't aware that a seed from my coaching tree had just blossomed. He used the same terminology: "Vermont" was our zone offense, and he stressed ball reversal on offense and help side on defense. In 2015 his team won the middle school championship. Frankie, Tyree, and Cris were on that team. Each one had certain adjustments to make to the high school game. Frankie was seamless and started as a freshman, Ty needed a year to grow, and Cris didn't even try out his freshman year. He couldn't get an appointment for a physical. We were disappointed that Cris didn't play for us last year, but we understood. His father had recently died of a heart attack. It was a difficult period for Cris.

This was what I had always wanted: kids entering high school cognizant of the fundamentals of basketball. Year after year, I would get kids who could dunk but couldn't pivot. They would shoot with the palms of their hands instead of their fingertips. Gaby helped mold three very good players, and by sophomore year all three had a supporting role on the team.

Gaby, fluent in Spanish and a Bronx native, was able to talk to Frankie's, Ty's, and Cris's parents. They trusted him. His status as an alumnus and former player held a lot of stock. He is a guide. Sometimes the players feel overwhelmed, and he provides assistance to them.

This year we had expected the three best players from Gaby's team to join us at the high school, but then the Catholic schools stepped in and recruited them away. Funding for the middle school team also disappeared. Without coaching responsibilities, Gaby joined the bench as a full-time assistant coach for the first time this season.

The market for talented middle school basketball players

has always been closed to us. The schools with AAU connections and sneaker contracts attract most of the talented middle school stars. They are mosquitoes among bats—they get quickly gobbled up. Some schools collect player after player indiscriminately. It reminds me of when the Bronx legend Rod Strickland reportedly said he didn't want to be another horse in University of North Carolina coach Dean Smith's stable. Perception is everything.

TYREE RISING

Even without recruiting we were doing fine. Even without Frankie we were doing fine. Actually, we were doing fantastic. The next game, against Metropolitan High School, Tyree erupted for 27 points and 8 rebounds. Then he broke the school record for points, 43, in the next game against Archimedes. He had nine three-pointers, also a school record. Eureka! He had finally discovered his stroke.

I tried to get us ready for Bathgate. I felt like we were heading for a trap. Tyree had just had one of the best shooting performances I had ever seen. We were due for a letdown.

During warm-ups against Bathgate, Ty looked as confident as a kid who just scored 43 points would and was basking in his newfound confidence. I thought he was paying more attention to who was in the crowd than to what his teammates were doing, but then I noticed he was giving a pound and high five to every single one of his teammates.

We beat Bathgate 76–48. Tyree dropped an impressive 27 points. He had worked his way back and excelled without

Frankie. He became the glue the team needed after Frankie's injury. Crazy thing was, he almost transferred last season. He was recruited by the same school that tried to get Charles to transfer two years ago. The bigger high schools in New York City are always recruiting. Imagine a gymnasium filled with a dozen of what my uncle Richie would call *omadhauns,* or fools. Sitting next to them would be several lapsed Catholics from Queens, a couple of AAU hucksters, and a few former hardwood titans wearing drawstring shorts. These older men had been recruited themselves to tell lies to naively optimistic young men, their fishbowl bellies floating around the gym, their polo shirts screaming their allegiance to their high school. These overlords are part of the industry. They hustled too much and worked too little, but there was always movement of talented kids between schools. The talent of New York City basketball is in the hands of a chosen few. You could call them oligarchs. All are filled with *naglost,* the Russian word describing arrogance, chutzpah, or the lack of civility.

Gaby called Tyree's mom in for a meeting. She was on our side. It was quite easy to convince him that Fannie Lou was his home. I also discovered that Tyree's father was not a strong presence in his life. This left Ty feeling angry and vulnerable. There's not a lot I can do with unsolicited confessions about missing dads, wayward moms, incarcerated older brothers, nieces without vaccinations, ACS cases, wrongdoings at the shelter. But I try.

I don't have a large window of time to work with these guys. Four years, at most, is not a lot of time. I like to take freshmen and put them on varsity. I want four-year players because it takes time to teach them the game of basketball and good habits like nutrition and sleep. In the summer, we go to basketball camp at local colleges. For most, it is the first time they are on a college campus for an extended period of time.

One of the best ways I can help guys like Tyree and Shamar

and Cris grow is through structured practices, in-depth film sessions, statistics. We can discuss how they are playing. Most freshmen think I am being cruel when I talk about what they can and cannot do. They usually adjust around their junior years to the criticism or feedback. It looks like Ty is ahead of the curve this year. He recognizes it not as criticism, but as help. Their relationship with feedback is in direct correlation with how much they trust me. Feedback can help them grow as players. Trust helps them grow as men. And that is why I coach: to build young men.

When it comes to coaching, I am clearly a Benthamite. Jeremy Bentham thought happiness came when you avoided pain. I see losses as causing pain, so I try to avoid them as much as I can. I've managed to avoid too many losses by preparing not to lose. Through scouting, I try as much as I can to teach the team about what could happen in the game. We are always very prepared. I don't want my team ever to feel I didn't prepare them for a game or a situation. I don't want to let them down, and they don't want to let me down. So far so good.

THE JELLY

Tyree was not the only one playing well. Jaelen, the freshman, handled his launch into the starting lineup well. His hands and feet were sometimes poorly positioned, as is often the case with freshmen—a drag of the pivot foot here, an untimely drive there. He lacked the typical resourcefulness of a seasoned varsity player, yet he had the doggedness of a lost cabdriver determined to find his way. JB was juggling a lot. He had schoolwork, a girlfriend, and after school he was responsible for his younger brother and sister. He would run up the street, pick them up, and bring them to practice. They would do their homework in the bleachers.

The biggest surprise of the season was Shamar. Against Alfred E. Smith High School, Shamar had a career-high 32 points. He did not look hampered in his new role. In fact, he looked freaking awesome. Shamar's nickname, "Mr. Give Me Lane," held true tonight. He attacked the rim fearlessly. His coterie of friends with similar names, Mr. Greenlight and Mr. You Can't Guard Me, would have been proud of Shamar tonight.

Shamar had almost perfected "the jelly": a finger roll in its inception, the ball would roll off his hand, and the move would conclude with a little flare, a kick off the leg, or a deceptive spin off the glass. As he finished the move you could hear the bench and the crowd say, "Jelly." It was a viral move. Considering the talents of New York City guards, it is difficult not only to create a new move, but to market it as well. The Jelly comes packaged for anyone to try. Unlike the dunk, something that most of us cannot do, the Jelly is not utilitarian; it is aesthetic. A bold layup with a piquant finish—it sounds like a coffee commercial. It gets the crowds caffeinated. It is not the iconic George Gervin finger roll, where he floated like a statue toward the rim and if you blinked you missed seeing his hand release the ball like a magician. The Jelly is a refined finger roll with an assassin's heart. Tyree and Shamar will sometimes look their defender in the eye, as if they are telling them they are going to Jelly and there isn't a damn thing they can do about it.

Started by a few guards in New York City, it was the move of the year. Ty liked it. Shamar embraced it. Sometimes it didn't work, like in traffic. It was best served on a fast break one-on-one.

After the game, Shamar was the last one to leave the room. Soaking up the career-high endorphins. I was proud of him. He had worked very hard on his game and was now reaping the results.

"Great game. You are really playing well," I said.

"I felt like I had to not only worry about my spot on the floor, but to make sure everyone was in position to get a bucket. I'm already a nervous person, so that became even more nerve-racking," Shamar confessed. "Coach, get home safe."

"You too."

SPIES LIKE US

Anastasia Bitis, the brilliant Maspeth coach, filmed the Bathgate game in a clandestine fashion. This may seem like blatant espionage, but there's really nothing wrong with filming your opponent. We all do it. As coaches, we teach during the day and somehow are able to find time to develop a couple of lesson plans for our real job, the one that pays us. After school we somehow find the time to develop another two-hour lesson plan: fifteen minutes of shooting drills, twenty minutes of shell defense, full-court press defense and offense, special situations, free throws, zone sets, man-to-man sets, sideline out-of-bounds plays, baseline out-of-bounds plays. The *really* dedicated scout opponents and watch film.

The Maspeth Argonauts, located in Maspeth, Queens, were 9-1, their lone loss coming to South Bronx Prep. They were also ranked as one of the top ten teams in New York State polls, and every year are ranked as a contender for the city championship. The 2015 PSAL Class B champs, Maspeth have been on our non-conference schedule since they knocked us out of the playoffs that year. After some teams win a high school championship, they crumble back to earth and aren't as potent anymore. Schools like Maspeth keep climbing. Maspeth has a wonderful basketball program.

The sunlit Maspeth gym awoke a wicked memory of a recent painful defeat: Bari Higinio and Ken Duran's last game, and the sad end of the *New York Times* story. When I closed my eyes, *the massacre at Maspeth* glowed on my internal film screen. The autopsy continued to haunt me. I have watched that game at least twenty times. It still feels like Maspeth didn't miss a shot that night.

When we entered the gym, "Hate Me Now" by Nas filled the air. Maspeth players were warming up, waiting, aggressively impatient, on a Wednesday afternoon three days after Christmas. They looked at us like we drank all the eggnog.

"I don't think they have ever lost here," Gaby said. "Look." He pointed to several green, white, and blue banners displaying several undefeated seasons.

My heart sank.

I tried to erase the bitter memory of *The Game*—the 2015 playoff loss to Maspeth. Michael Powell and the impeccable photographer Todd Heisler captured us at our most vulnerable, a playoff loss. Sure, last year we beat Maspeth quite easily at Fannie Lou in front of twenty people. Actually, I turned last year's game on the other day. Maspeth's guards could not bring the ball up against Kobe Boateng and Frankie's defense. I missed the verve Kobe and Frankie created on defense last year. They were unsubtle thieves, removing the ball like a gang of Gypsies wearing neon T-shirts advertising their intentions to pickpocket you. Frankie and Kobe specialized in this brand of thievery. I had to turn the game off.

As usual, Charles won the jump and Shamar blew by the lone defender for an easy layup on the left side. We hadn't seen anything like Maspeth's half-court defense this year. It was apparent to me that they had studied us well. After a few more possessions, I wondered if they knew what we had for breakfast, the last movie I watched, what photos I liked on Instagram.

It was clear this rivalry was becoming like a Cold War spy novel. We knew each other's secrets. No team plays harder than Maspeth, so how do you beat them? There was a superpower tension right here in ironclad industrial Maspeth, Queens.

In the second quarter, Maspeth switched to a three-quarter-court trapping 1–2–2 defense.

"Look familiar?" Gaby asked me.

"Anastasia was at the Bathgate game and it worked well for us. Why not?"

A brilliant cloak-and-dagger move: use your enemy's best defense on them. It worked well against us. Forced a few turnovers. We were forced to call a time-out.

"Get into Wildcat," I instructed. Our press offense.

Eyes nodded. Their heads stood still like statues in the huddle. "This game is about effort, the effort to come to a pass, to sprint to your spot, to know what the hell to do when you are out on the court," I said irritably.

Once up by twelve, we barely survived a stormy second quarter to be down five, 30–25. My youth brigade acted like they had their passwords changed on them and kept repeating the same old password until Maspeth was back into the game. The Argos had their own Enigma Machine and had deciphered our plays.

At halftime we walked to the dreaded locker room. I recalled it had the same temperature as a meat locker. I stared at the halftime statistics. Only Charles and Walfri had rebounds.

"Damn."

I grabbed the handle. It was locked. "Now I don't even have a proper place to get mad."

Annoyance turned into fury.

Turnovers! Shamar performed like he was playing for Maspeth. He had only one assist and one bucket.

"Mack, you keep dribbling into the trap. Reverse the ball."

At this point, my voice was echoing up and down the staircase. Mack's encyclopedic knowledge of basketball was always impressive, but at times, on the court, it would leave him.

"If you don't have it, get it going to somebody else, please." I modulated the roar into a more didactic voice.

"JB, you're hanging out at half-court while everyone is trying to rebound. Please get your butt in there and rebound."

"What's your middle name, Tyree?"

"Ronald."

"You sure? I want to make sure they didn't kidnap you or give us the Tyree clone."

Maspeth had Tyree in a chokehold. He was in a different universe from that 43-point game. He had 7 points and wouldn't score in the second half.

As is true of many halftime rants, this one seemed to cut down our mistakes as much as increase our advantages. Games like these are a test of a team's character.

Tied late in the fourth, we needed a bucket. We also needed a play Maspeth hadn't seen. They knew everything; our cover was blown. I sketched the scene. I had seen the Denver Nuggets run this one a few times. Implementing the enshrined act of misdirection, Ty would set two screens.

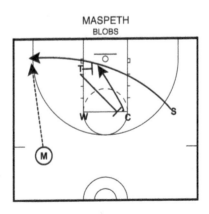

MASPETH
BLOBS

"Tyree, you're on the left block, you will screen for Shamar. Shamar, Ty is going to screen for Charles. Give the ball to him. Charles, if you get doubled, look to kick it out. If not, go to work." Good coaching has a little sorcery and deception and a lot of forgery in it. They ran the play perfectly. Charles scored on the layup. Time-out Maspeth. Out of the time-out, Shamar got a steal. He passed to Walfri. He cut right and, like a quarterback delivering the ball to his trusted fullback for a third-and-inches, handed Shamar the ball. Walfri's defender threw himself on top of Shamar for what looked to be a loss of yards on the play. If it was football that was what it would have looked like, but in basketball you can't tackle a player. A foul was called.

Shamar calmly went to the line. He took his patented dribble sequence.

"Hey, Lil Uzi, don't miss!" some clever fan from the crowd yelled.

Swish.

Shamar went to the line for his second shot.

The crowd needed to try something that might throw Shamar off.

"Travis Scott."

This one hit some rim, but same result.

"Gaby, who are Travis Scott and Lil Uzi?" I asked.

"Two rappers that have hair like Shamar." Gaby giggled.

It didn't matter what the crowd yelled. Shamar was 6-for-6 from the free-throw line in the fourth quarter. We won 66–63.

There was more good news: Walfri's hardheadedness from early on in the season had disappeared like the morning mist on the Hudson River. Walfri and Charles had 10 blocks. We usually shackled teams on the perimeter; today, numbers 3 and 34 defended the paint well.

And so, after surviving the Maspeth game, a weight was lifted off our shoulders, a weight we could finally put away. I do believe in revenge games. I believe in packing away ghosts. Ghosts linger around basketball, and the best way to get rid of them is to beat them. It was Maspeth's first loss at home in their brief, but extremely successful, three-year varsity program history.

Charles told a local reporter, "It feels pretty good. Our team really stuck together. They are our rivals and this gives us more confidence as we get ready to go into the playoffs."

Dear Charles, it is December 28, and the playoffs are two months away with a lot of basketball to play. Nonetheless, we were undefeated for the second year in a row on New Year's Eve because of Shamar's clutch free throws.

It is difficult to exaggerate how important Shamar has become to the team. He embodies the season's undertow of determination, of never quitting. Our once-vexed relationship had become one of reliability and trust.

We jogged to our white chariot of a minibus. Shamar had his arm around Kaleb.

"I got cut twice because I was a dribble-head," Shamar confessed. "I thought I could impress everyone with my quickness and dribbles. Listen to Coach now, it will make your life easier." Shamar was sharing his wisdom and the rock thoughtfully.

FRANKIE'S LEG

In our first game back from the holiday break, we didn't miss a beat. In fact, after the few days off we looked rejuvenated.

In a flash the Comprehensive Model High School game arrived. Their away Carolina-blue uniforms were a welcome surprise. I examined the bench. Kenneth looked unusually nervous.

It was his birthday, and his friends in the stands had reminded me several times to try to get him in the game. Frankie, in street clothes, milled about awkwardly at the far end of the bench. His crutches took up space we didn't have. We attacked them like a virus and the score grew exponentially: 11–0. We would score and then our 2–2–1 zone press would turn deadly; a month ago it was benign.

Shamar's pressure forced another steal, and he delivered it to Charles for a hoop plus the foul.

CMHS's coach reminded his players, "George, George!"

A chorus of "George, George!" rings out from our players.

We may or may not know their play, but we will always call it out like we know it. It messes with our opponents' heads.

In the Maspeth game we had a difficult time executing on offense, but tonight everyone was locked in. Tonight Shamar's passes had the precision of a *mohel*. He would drive into the paint and deliver the ball on time and on target to Charles time after time. Charles was wearing a white headband that pressed his hair up like a head of broccoli. At one point in the second quarter, he stole an errant pass and drove toward the hoop. A defender was running parallel on his right. Next Charles executed a perfect Fibonacci sequence, wrapping the ball around his hip like Oscar Robertson, then elevating and incredibly dunking the ball with his right hand. It was a phenomenal play. For an encore at the end of the second quarter, Charles tried a windmill dunk that ricocheted off the back of the rim. We walked toward Room 103 for halftime incubation.

"Are you mad at me?" Charles asked.

"Why would I be mad at you?" We were up twenty-five points at halftime.

"Because I missed the dunk."

"Yeah. I am. Don't do that again. I mean, miss."

In the third quarter, Charles made a Jerry Stackhouse–esque dunk. He was having a good time. All of us were.

Kenneth, the birthday boy, subbed in the fourth quarter. Charles ended the night with 33 points and 24 rebounds in a little over three quarters. Tyree had 28 points. Immediately Kenneth tried to score. He missed two wide-open threes. We were up 92–52, and on the last possession the crowd was begging him to shoot, but he politely and respectfully dribbled out the clock.

After the game we met in my room.

"Yo, yo, stop getting dressed." There was always a warning in Ty's voice.

I kept the postgame talk short. The guys threw their jerseys in the large red duffel bag. Each one shuffled out. Kenneth was last. He looked sad.

"Why didn't you shoot it?" I asked.

"Coach, you told us not to score on the last possession if we are up. It is disrespectful."

"You're right, Kenneth. Happy birthday."

Not all was well. Midway through the third, I had looked down the bench and realized Frankie had headphones on and looked to be listening to music.

"What the hell are you doing?"

He quickly removed them and tucked them away.

The better we were playing, the further Frankie was drifting away from us. Even though he was only a few feet from us, it was the furthest he'd ever been from the team. The fracture in his foot was healing, but another one was clearly forming as we kept winning without him. We were worried about his foot healing, but we should have been watching his heart. He wanted to escape. This was painful for me. I remember wanting to escape. I remember trying to escape.

Sitting on the bench was killing Frankie. It was hurting his mother too. She hadn't been to a game since the injury. She told me she just couldn't see him sit on the bench injured.

Even if Frankie did return this season, it was unlikely he

would be the same player. He had been off to such a great start, and recapturing your poise, confidence, conditioning, and feel for the game in February is about as unlikely as recovering a stolen bike in New York City. Once your bike is gone, it is gone. Once the season is gone, you can't recover it. Frankie's season was over even if he came back. I should have done a better job of making him feel a part of the team.

APOPLECTIC

I've been asked a hundred times why I get so angry when I'm coaching. There has never been a reassuringly comprehensible answer. I would say, "I'm trying to get their attention! I'm trying to control the chaos of the game with my voice! Have you ever practiced something and asked someone to perform it and they forget it seconds after you just told them?" These attempts never really satisfy anyone. My answers are ungratifying, lacking some fundamental reason behind my anger. In some way this is my biggest failure as a coach, the ability not to lose my mind. My second-biggest failure is my inability to convince people that I'm not really angry. Nonetheless, I aspire to coach without looking angry. These two ideals seem opposed—coaching successfully without yelling—but they are both the byproduct of expectations. I'm sure you are still not satisfied with my explanation.

Maybe the error is in the question "Why are you so angry?" I'm not angry. I may look frustrated or hysterical. Can I request a concession? Can we agree I am coaching with passion? It means I care. It means my players are very committed to the team. I see this compromise pleases nobody. Yelling is clearly a way to seize control when I feel helpless. When we adjust our offense or press to whatever I was yelling about, my intensity decreases. Do I lie in bed with anguish after a loss? Yes. Is basketball an obsessive pursuit? It has turned out that way. I don't think it's destructive. The game without a coach's displeasure, anger, frustration, rage, irritation is just a pickup game. A carefree exercise.

I see the contradiction in coaching. We mold and shape young minds and then scream at them for a mistake or a temporary lapse in judgment. Isn't it necessary to correct someone? I yell not in order to embarrass, but to recalibrate. My displeasure is a form of discipline and a sharp reminder to get back on defense. Sometimes it is for show. I know I need to help my players focus on the next play and not dwell on some lost moment like a dropped pass or an ill-timed cut. But there is also the key concept of mindfulness: I want them to be aware not to make the same mistake again. So I may look apoplectic on the sideline as I try to amplify our talent in the middle of a fierce competition.

Sometimes it is the cumulative casualties of the game that make me look like a certified madman. The errors add up until I spill over in a cascade of screams. I've searched for more congenial ways of coaching. I haven't found one.

I hear all the time, "Why are you yelling when you are up by thirty points?" But don't conflate yelling with degrading. It's like a cognitive awakening. An alarm clock. Great basketball teams talk on defense and offense. When they forget to talk, I remind them, sometimes loudly.

I have been given medical advice: "Watch your blood pressure." Or even a prognosis: "You're going to have an aneurysm." People have commented on the colors of my face: from warm pink after a turnover, to tomato red after an egregiously poor shot, and finally badly sunburned after a loss.

When the San Antonio Spurs held Tim Duncan's retirement ceremony, his coach Gregg Popovich said, "If your superstar can take a little hit now and then, everybody else can shut the hell up and fall in line." The sentence really struck me, because this season Charles, Tyree, Walfri, Shamar, and Frankie can all take what Popovich called a "hit." Popovich continued by saying, "Thank you for letting me coach you, Timmy. I'm really thankful because you allowed me to coach the team." I couldn't have said it better. Charles, Tyree, and Frankie walked into the building allowing me to coach them. Walfri and Shamar took some time, but by senior year they were ready. Popovich's words reminded me to thank my team for allowing me to coach them. I am deeply grateful to have a team as committed as they are.

For me, coaching has always felt cathartic. It becomes a relief to pace about theatrically up and down the sidelines. When things go our way it feels good, but it can be stressful and exhausting when they don't. We all should be more pliable in life; things are not going to go our way all the time. However, sometimes in the midst of a game, it is as if I can see the play before it happens: *No. Don't throw that pass!*

There may be no good answers to the question of anger. My coaching is fueled by a deep desire to win and also to achieve the precision to execute a play where the optimal time, a blink of an eye, lasts half a second. It all depends on the angle of the screen, the velocity and location of the pass, the speed of the cut, the spin off the glass. After we miss four straight layups, it isn't out of character for me to stomp my feet on the ground, vexed by the weird breaks of this game. Or to blame the refs, their flawed and faulty interpretations of the game, sending me into a fit of internal combustion.

Coaching is not just about yelling. We are after all just a team, built not on talent alone, but on a committed brotherhood. Each team is constructed on a harshly complex system of plays. Each year we have players who are brand-new, and it takes them months and sometimes years to understand what is going on at Fannie Lou.

I know I fail to give a satisfying answer about my own inability to quietly coach, but please know I am trying. Truth be told, I would like to stay calm. It's the goal of every committed, passionate coach trying to get the best out of his or her players at every moment of the game. So the final thing I want to say about anger while coaching hoops is this: I don't want to lose.

THE SHARK MASSACRE: SOUTH BRONX PREP, GAME NUMBER ONE

In the second week of January, for the first time in school history Fannie Lou Hamer Freedom High School was ranked number one in the state in Class B. I was afraid to let the team know. We had four games scheduled that week, and it felt more like a distraction than a reward. Nonetheless, we easily cruised through the games that week. Monday we beat the Bronx School for Law, Government and Justice by 27. Shamar had a triple-double, and Charles had 27 points and 21 rebounds. Wednesday was a 51-point victory over Bronx Leadership Academy in which we unearthed Cris Reyes and he hit four consecutive three-pointers. Could Cris be ready to get into the rotation before the playoffs? Gaby loved Cris's relentlessness on offense. I loved his wolverine's instinct on defense.

My favorite story about Cris was one Gaby kept telling me over and over again during tryouts: "In middle school this kid hit him with a nasty crossover. Made Cris touch the floor. He didn't care. He bounced right back up like nothing happened." I'm a fan of this type of determination and toughness. Cris deserved effusive praise, as the whole team did for their commitment and hard work. At this point in the season we adapted the Latin phrase *Per angusta ad augusta*—"Through difficulty to greatness"—as our motto. Cris was an embodiment of this phrase. He had worked very hard over the last few months. In an era when everyone uses social media as a platform to let the world know how hard they are working, Cris's determination to get on the court was admirably demonstrated in silence. Which fits his personality. He was an almost silent kid. He rarely spoke. When Cris was in the eighth grade, his father died of a heart attack. At times I felt as if Cris was silent because he was in mourning.

Friday night we knocked out Frederick Douglass Academy III by thirty-five. All five starters scored in double digits. The winning streak had extended to sixteen. Pardon my literary license for a minute, but consider what Leo Tolstoy meant when he wrote, "If you look for perfection, you'll never be content." We were a perfect 16–0 and very happy. Kids in the school were comparing us to the Golden State Warriors. There was a palpable excitement about our streak. We weren't chasing perfection. We were here to work; we knew perfection would always be out of our grasp. The excitement even went beyond the walls of the school. It traveled across the city. This was not artificial. It was real. Everyone knew. When I picked up Nina from school, there was an excited dad who wanted to brag and make me laugh that his daughter was also undefeated in chess. He wished us good luck, and I reciprocated.

It was Saturday's game that we were thinking about all week. The battle of the last two unbeaten teams in New York State, Fannie Lou and South Bronx Prep. It felt like a once-in-a-decade game. I woke up early on Saturday. In the dark, I slalomed gracefully, avoiding vagabond Legos and the creaky spots in the floor. The wood floor gives us splinters, sometimes splinters so big we have to make visits to the emergency room to get them removed. I made a cup of coffee and watched last year's South Bronx Prep game.

They were a different team this year. They were on a different planet. They had also cruised this week, winning games by scores of 121–18, 129–76, and 110–29! Those scores were meant to intimidate. They were menacing.

The Martin Luther King, Jr. Tournament at Monroe High School—yes, the same Monroe that helped give birth to Fannie Lou Hamer Freedom High School—was hosting one of the premier games of the 2016–17 basketball season. Last year we'd beaten SBP in overtime. This year, with a glitch in the scheduling, we weren't scheduled to play each other in conference play. We had beaten SBP thirteen times and lost twice, but those two losses had come within the last four years. So something was brewing.

The winner would be the top seed in the citywide playoffs and enjoy bragging rights. The gym was filled with students, alumni, reporters, coaches, and a few people who did not necessarily love Fannie Lou. I spotted Steven, the school custodian, with his children. My friend Chris and his son Emile were in attendance, and my buddy Brent even drove down from Boston to catch the game. And Molly Shabica was there.

Molly, our ultra-talented science teacher, brought her family to this tournament each year. I owe a lot to Molly. She was directly responsible for getting me the job at Fannie Lou. We were classmates in graduate school, and she mentioned that her school needed a teacher. In the summer of 2003 I got the job. With her husband, Tank, and their two sons in tow, I greeted them and thanked them for coming.

"This team scores a lot of points," I said. "I hope to slow them down."

Our defensive hallmark was to keep teams under 40 points a game. Our pace and scoring had increased this year, but the numbers that South Bronx Prep was putting up were prodigious. They were unblinkingly running up the score on a bunch of glass-jaw victims. How does a team average almost 105 points in a thirty-two-minute game? Could we slow them down?

Time for the main event. Charles, in the black trunks, entered into the circle at half-court. The crowd reached for their phones. He was met in the circle by his nemesis, Ali Sumerah, wearing the white trunks. Their respective teammates surrounded them; there was electricity in the air: number 3 versus number 3. Eleventh grader versus eleventh grader. Charles and Ali stood toe to toe, nose to nose, pound for pound. In the tale of the tape, Ali may have had an inch or two over Charles.

Countless cell phones recorded the jump ball. The court was so strangely photogenic—the sunlight honey-colored the gym, it was what photographers call the Golden Hour—that I could be forgiven for thinking that the spectators, if not the coaches, were really going to enjoy this game. The ball sailed upward and Ali tipped it to his point guard, Tilquan Rucker. Rucker led the PSAL in scoring at 38 points a game. He *averaged* a triple-double, even though he stood at five feet five inches in high-tops. Charles wasn't even in the top ten in scoring in the PSAL, but he had become one of the best rebounders in the city because of his competitive fire. The fans shifted, now occupied with Instagramming their photos.

Charles had a crown, a symbolic gesture for his friend Prince, sketched with a magic marker on the fleshy part of his hand between the thumb and index finger. He has been feasting on the competition all year, but tonight he had company at the table. He had to share those rebounds with Ali today. On this chilly Saturday in January, he was allowing Ali to seal him early, often, and deep in the paint. Rebounds he normally grabbed were being stolen by Ali.

Charles picked up boxing when he was eleven to deal with his parents' separation. He eventually stopped because he didn't like to hurt people, but even though he doesn't box anymore he continues to have a fighter's mentality, as if every rebound belongs to him. Coming into the season, Charles began using the hashtag #HuntingSeason on his Twitter account.

I asked him what it meant. "We are hunting for a championship," he said.

Charles first dunked a basketball when he was eleven. He made the varsity basketball team when he was fourteen, his freshman year. His first year in high school he had several impressive dunks, but had a difficult time doing the other important things in basketball, like dribbling, shooting, pivoting, and passing. Over the years I have had a lot of players rely on an athleticism that allowed them to ignore the subtleties of the game. Charles was an exception. He was blossoming in real time. By the end of his freshman season, he had become a serious student of the game of basketball, and in his first-ever playoff game he recorded a double-double. Each season he steadily improved. His sophomore season he averaged 12 points and 7 rebounds a game. This year he was averaging 20 points and 14 rebounds a game. No team had had an answer for Charles this season. Until now.

On the opposite sideline stood the South Bronx Prep coach, Paul Campbell. Paul grew up not too far from James Monroe High School in the Bronx River Houses complex. He looked pleased, like he had invited everyone and they all showed up. He was an articulate, intelligent young man who some thought suffered from a certain self-aggrandizement. And why not? His team was really, really good. Coach Paul was otherwise known as Radar, in my opinion the coolest nickname ever. (For a coach, at least.) He needed a car to fit his nickname. It wasn't like a guy named Radar could drive a minivan or a bicycle to school. Paul drove around in a white Mercedes. He was by far the best-dressed coach in the PSAL. (Today, though, he and his coaching staff were dressed in matching blue tracksuits.)

His Instagram posts were a hive of hashtags—#ontheRadar, #ChipChasing—and emojis of a basketball and a trophy, a bull's-eye, a red "100" symbol, and a flexing black bicep. He typed, "You can't rewrite what's already been written" in his latest Instagram post of himself wearing a union blue T-shirt saying "Talent Wins Games, Teamwork Wins Chips." I thought of a line from Jean-Luc Godard: "Europeans have memories, Americans have T-shirts."

The Monroe High School gym wasn't decorated with the typical bric-a-brac. The walls were white and yellow. The court was the kind of generic high school court that we rarely play on. By the size of the crowd, it looked like everyone wanted to see the battle of the last two undefeated teams in the Empire State. I haven't ever seen a crowd this large for a Fannie Lou regular-season game. The gym was loud. A friend's dad after the game would comment that it had a strange smell: a combination of marijuana and sweat.

We knew the South Bronx Prep Cougars would use a full-court press, and we planned to attack. On our first possession Ty went up, and their power forward, sophomore Jordan Agyemang, inhaled the ball out of Ty's hands. On the next possession JB tried attacking the paint, and Rucker spiked it out of bounds with two hands. They had set the stage. We were just going up and shooting contested layups—no moves, no fakes, no jukes, no hesitations. We were like the inept dancers at the wedding doing the same move over and over again all night.

Ty drove the ball and kicked it to a wide-open JB for a three. He nailed it. It was a big shot from the freshman, but teams like SBP aren't knocked out in the first quarter. "Great shot, JB," I said.

JB got caught dreaming about his bucket and left Rucker open for a three five feet behind the line.

"He leads the city in scoring, you cannot lose him!" I screamed at JB as if I were an alarm clock.

Rucker was the kind of player who had unlimited range plus unlimited confidence, an intoxicating combination. Like Charles, Rucker also improved each season. Like Charles, Rucker (five-five!) could also dunk. Unlike Charles, Rucker would shoot from anywhere on the court, anytime. We were down at the end of the first quarter, 16–14. We had given up 13 points on layups alone. Our offensive mistakes allowed them easy points.

There was a great pass from Ty to Walfri on a nicely executed sideline out-of-bounds play. But today Ty had trouble holding on to the ball. He looked nervous. He was 0-for-4 from the field. Nonetheless, with a couple of put-backs by the indefatigable Charles, we were able to tie the game at 18.

But every time we were about to get some momentum, we lost our footing. Walfri picked up his third foul midway through the second quarter, and in a flash we were down ten, 28–18. This is how South Bronx Prep killed teams, because other teams could not take care of the ball, because other teams could not play transition defense. They kept picking off our passes in the half-court sets. This was Blitzkrieg Basketball. *Vernichtungsschlacht.* They were about to annihilate us.

Bryant, Walfri's substitution, wasn't sure of the play and missed setting a screen for Tyree. Bryant's hair was meticulous and his defense was usually stellar, but today he too seemed a little tentative. On the next possession we had a chance to run the same sidelines out-of-bounds play that has become quite efficient for us over the years. I subbed Bryant out and went smaller with Mack. Mack, the backup point guard now converted to our backup power forward, also forgot to set the screen. We needed to execute if we were going to win. Or at least put up a fight. It was as if Charles with a miss and a put-back was our best offense so far.

I cursed as Tyree just threw it to a SBP defender with one

minute and forty-six seconds left in the half. I wanted to deliver a soliloquy on *unforced turnovers*. Now we are still down ten, in danger of being pummeled. It didn't look good. This was what the Cougars have done to every team they have played this year.

We needed a time-out. As the team jogged to our bench, I didn't need to look at the stats. I had seen all our turnovers with my eyes. We had fifteen turnovers already. I started punching the blue three-ring binder into submission. I erupted into a vortex of advice, threats, and supplication.

"On every pass you have to meet the damned ball!"

"You have to set screens on people, not air."

My right hand was slapping my left palm, making the same sound a beaver's tail does when it smacks a tranquil lake.

"Every pass, you meet it."

"That's it!"

I stomp on the floor to exaggerate what we need to do. The gym went silent. I try to coach without being angry, but we weren't fighting and I wanted to fight the whole gym.

Coming out of the time-out, Shamar hit a three on a smart pass from Tyree. Then a defensive stop and Ty grabbed the rebound and found JB for a driving layup. His shot wasn't falling today, but he was making things easier for his teammates. Only down five. We had survived a few haymakers.

The end of the first half was coming to a close, yet nobody on our team wanted to shoot. We must have made twenty passes, exhausting the seconds and the South Bronx Prep defense simultaneously.

"What are you waiting for?" I screamed as the seconds ticked away.

Mack answered me by hitting a three on the right wing at the buzzer. We were down only four, 32–28, at halftime.

Frankie, wearing a red Panthers T-shirt, clapped loudly as we headed to the locker room. He had the look in his eye that he wanted to play. At some point during the game, he had put his jersey on over his street clothes. Whatever happened today, Frankie's absence on the court was an ominous asterisk sitting next to me. Nonetheless, we had a good start to the third quarter. Shamar short-rimmed a quick three, but Walfri, our Al Horford/Kevin McHale/Kurt Rambis/Horace Grant, the bluest-collar guy we have, picked it up and put it back in to cut the lead to 35–32. We were doing a great job of slowing down SBP's hyper-explosive offense. Ty finally hit a three-pointer from the right corner to make it 37–35.

Charles drove down the lane and passed it to Ty for what would have been our first lead since the first quarter, but Ty air-balled it. He got a haircut a few days ago and hasn't been the same since. I wish his barber would go on vacation for the rest of the season.

Each team was battling. On consecutive possessions Rucker came down and got a hoop plus the foul, and Charles returned the favor with his own fiery "and-one" dunk above a storm of arms and elbows. Down by only one point. The crowd knew they were watching a classic.

"Yeah, Charles! We got this! They can't stop you!" Frankie yelled.

Trash talking can have the inverse effect. It can motivate your opponent. On the very next possession, Rucker came down and nailed a three. He scanned the bench, made eye contact with Frankie, and put his finger to his lip: "Shh." At that moment Rucker reminded me of a young Sugar Ray Leonard: an angelic butcher of the hardwood. He was small and fierce and one heck of a player.

"Defense! Defense! Defense!" A chant of encouragement came from our corner.

Rucker plowed right into Walfri.

"That's an offensive foul!" I yelled. For once the ref and I agreed.

"Shoot the ball, Ty, shoot the ball!" I barked at Ty on the next possession.

He dribbled to his right to create a little bit more space. *Swish.* Great shooters are an obsessive bunch. They have a wolflike approach to basketball: they spend a lot of time alone. I have watched Tyree shoot with the lights off in the gym. On solitary mornings he would shoot hundreds of shots with an oversize basketball. A normal basketball has a circumference of 29.5 inches. Tyree shoots with a ball that has a circumference of 33 inches *every day.* His shot starts from his toes and ends at his fingers; great shooters prepare their feet as the ball approaches them. Some step into the pass, others will take a bunny hop as the ball meets their fingertips. Basketball is a palmless game: the ball never touches the middle part of your hand, the part where fortunes are told. Fingers and the bony part of your hand do all the work. As Ty catches the ball and springs upward, twisting slightly to his left, his feet swing in front of him. His elbow is near his eyebrow, and his hand now looks like a goose neck or as if he's holding a dead mackerel. He is the greatest shooter I have ever coached. It's uncanny for a sophomore to shoot this well. It looks as if every shot he takes is going in.

The game was tied 45–45. Time-out SBP. Two back-to-back layups by Ali and the lead went back up to four, 49–45. The crowd refused to sit and the gym slowly became standing-room-only. SBP stalled for the last shot of the third quarter, and here came Mark "The Hitman" Morgan, the senior guard, running baseline behind our zone.

"Ty, close out, you are giving him too much space," Frankie warned.

Swish.

The score was 54–48 at the end of three. That shot gave them the momentum. In between quarters, both teams looked exhausted.

"E-One coming out to start the fourth," I said.

I wanted to get Shamar going, and this backdoor play usually would help him gain some confidence. At times last season he would panic and forget some of the structured offense. Any parent of a teenager knows they forget to put away their clothes, headphones occasionally are misplaced, and absentmindedness is a rite of passage. Mistakes are mistakes. But this year Shamar had been excellent. Just not today. Shamar froze. He was supposed to go backdoor, but he just stood there. Charles waited and then waited a little bit longer for Shamar to cut, until he couldn't wait any longer. He sprung ahead, took one dribble, and punched another dunk over everyone.

I had never seen Charles like this. Remember when R2-D2 got his memory wiped clean when Darth Vader hit Luke's X-wing fighter? Luke had to do everything on his own. Charles was Luke today.

We were down four in the fourth, just like at Clinton in November.

"We got this!" Frankie yelled.

Charles picked up his fourth foul with seven minutes to go in the fourth. It was a kidney shot. He had to endure an energy-sapping stint on the bench. Without Charles, you could expect things to stagnate. Yet Mack found Shamar, in what can only be called an accidental offensive play, for a fast-break layup. Another miscue on offense, where the ball was fumbled and dropped, then poked and bounced away, was rescued when Walfri picked it up and splashed a beautiful mid-range jumper that cut the lead to two, 56–54. We got two consecutive defensive stops, and then, mysteriously, we threw the outlet back to SBP *twice*.

When we could get the ball over half-court, we were scoring, haphazardly and with not quite perfect execution, but we were getting the job done. Walfri had a beautiful spin move from the high post.

Charles reentered the game with 4:43 to go with four fouls, and we were down only three, 59–56. He was fouled going to the basket. He made one, missed the second one. If there was one weakness today, it was his free throws.

On offense the Cougars just stood around and watched Rucker miss another contested jumper. Ty gathered the rebound and nonchalantly threw it back to Mack. Out of nowhere the Cougars senior Danny Ramos, the Roberto Duran of this game, instinctively intercepted the pass. He tripped over Mack's foot, spun around as if he was in a cyclonic swirl, and flung the ball up toward the hoop. As he landed, the whistle blew; he scored a heartbreaking layup plus the foul. Knockout. Experience, traditionally overvalued in high school sports, was raised to an art form on that play—an incredible play only a senior could make.

We would not get off the canvas this time. Danny's play was like getting hit by those *manos de piedra*. It stove our boat. Sure, there was 3:38 remaining in the game, but we were dazed and swimming without our ship. We'd been swimming with sharks all along. Although with 1:20 remaining we cut the lead to four, a Rucker assist to Ramos for a three felt like a shark biting our leg off.

The classic purpose of a coach is always to appear calm, but I am rarely ever calm while on the sidelines. With a minute remaining, the game was slipping out of reach. Yelling at my seated crew, in the midst of some nonsensical basketball gibberish, I saw Ali clapping his hands at my madness. This was an intolerable provocation. We were already dead. Why dance on our corpse?

We lost 69–63.

"We were scared of serious competition," Charles said. This was one of the first times he had spoken critically of the team all season. Charles refused to spin the game. He knew and I knew there was something we could learn from today about ball security, toughness, competition, the big stage, free throws, life. It was important to learn from the loss and move on.

And that's what we did. We kept moving. But first we had to sit through the awards ceremony. Ty's, Shamar's, and Mack's jerseys hid their tears, Walfri's head was buried in a towel, Charles was stoic like a statue: all unambiguous images of defeat. This was a new form of torture: we were forced to watch our opponent celebrate with trophies and smiles at half-court.

"Look at them. Watch them get the awards. We will get them in March," I said.

Frankie sat, nodding. The rest were too teary-eyed to look up. A teenage girl in the stands seemed to be laughing at us at our most vulnerable. It was like in *Troilus and Cressida* when Cassandra's prophecy seemed to come true. She was a raving Cassandra, yelling,

"CRY, PANTHERS, CRY!"

Finally, we were freed from the shackles of the postgame celebration. In the locker room I may have punched a few lockers and promised again to beat SBP in March. I couldn't stop punching things: clipboards, my thigh, the locker, the red cushioned folding chair, the air. There's a scene in *Raging Bull* when Jake LaMotta, the Bronx Bull, will not stop punching the wall. That was me. I wanted to punch my way out of this game the way De Niro punches the wall, yelling, "Why? Why? Why?"

I remembered Ali clapping a little too close to the bench. I've lost all decorum, I thought.

Shakespeare and Scorsese may have captured the essence of the game of the decade, but I returned to Melville to help me with the loss. In Chapter 36, "The Quarter-Deck," after a few hundred pages we discover what happened to Ahab's leg: "Captain Ahab, I have heard of Moby-Dick—but it was not

Moby-Dick that took off thy leg?" South Bronx Prep had bitten off my leg, and I wanted revenge.

As we exited the locker room, a few local reporters asked us some questions. I felt like Ahab answering questions from his crew: "You were the number-one team in the state? Was it not South Bronx Prep that broke your jaw that ended your undefeated season? Hey, great game. You guys slowed them down. At least they didn't score a hundred on you." News reporters called it the game of the year.

The battle of the undefeateds left me exhausted and my jaw unhinged. It wasn't that the perfect season was ruined, it was the thought that South Bronx Prep might never lose a game that stayed with me. They were unbeatable. I thought I knew how to beat them, and I was wrong. The feeling of helplessness or of being wrong stung. The guys played their hearts out and more or less executed what I asked them to do. This wasn't a mutiny; the crew fought fiercely against these pirates of the hardwood, but to use another metaphor, I wasn't a surgeon carving up defenses, I was a dermatologist prescribing witch hazel for a ruptured gallbladder. I thought Frankie's injury was the nadir. I was wrong, twice.

A few hours after the game, I was still angry. *Still,* I could barely shut my mouth. I think my jaw was dislocated. I have this terrible habit of clenching my teeth during games. It's as if I am forcing my mandibles to fuse. I felt horrible after any loss, but this one hurt doubly.

The story of our loss was everywhere on social media. I wanted to tweet out, "Sure, we lost, but wait until we get Frankie back." Somehow I didn't. It was crucial the team understand this: we don't know if Frankie is coming back. I sat alone at home and thought about the game. How can we beat the Cougars? These Panthers have endured evictions, fear of getting jumped, absentee fathers, shootings, doubts about their immigrant status, an aggressive stop-and-frisk policy, drug-filled blocks, educational neglect, hunger, and domestic violence. In the grand scheme of things, this loss was minor. We'll get over this. *Per angusta ad augusta.*

We just needed a few days to heal. There's also something powerful about having Fannie Lou Hamer's name on our jerseys. It's like, *Fine, you won the game, but you really can't beat us because we are all Fannie Lou. We have her fighting spirit.*

FANNIE LOU HAMER

I have a strange and twisted relationship with South Bronx Prep. In December 2006 I won my first game ever as a head coach against them. There were lots of milestones that night. It was my first win and the school's first win in over two years. I don't remember any game details. What sticks with me from that night has nothing to do with the game itself. I can still hear the students in the stands, led by a young teacher, chanting, "Fannie Who? Fannie Who?" It was an attempt to intimidate us and mock the school, but in reality they were mocking a civil rights icon. I was reminded of what Nina Simone once said: "There's no excuse for the young people not knowing who the heroes and the heroines are or were." I wished those students had listened to her or even the talented Gil Scott-Heron. Gil's song "95 South" is an immensely moving song about Fannie Lou Hamer. My favorite line is: "Placed on this mountain with a rare chance to see. Dreams once envisioned by folks much braver than me."

Once you are done listening to Gil's song, you can listen to Fannie Lou Hamer herself on YouTube tell her own stories about what life was like in Mississippi. One such story I would like to share is when she was arrested in 1963. "We going to make you wish you were dead," the police said to her. Fannie Lou Hamer was escorted to a jail cell that was already occupied by two men. "I laid on my face and the first negro began to beat me . . . I was beat by the first negro until I was exhausted. The state highway patrolman ordered the second negro to take the blackjack." There are times when I can't tell if Americans purposely ignore history or if it is simply forgotten. But how can you forget about Mississippi?

Young adults from all over the United States went to Mississippi in 1964. It was the Freedom Summer movement, which Fannie Lou Hamer helped organize. The plan was to reveal to the world the hardships of Mississippi: the bigotry, the violence, the systematic exclusion of the black residents from schools and the voting booth, and the virulent fear of integration.

In June 1963, a year earlier, Mrs. Hamer had been detained at a rest stop in Sunflower County, Mississippi. Back at the jailhouse, she was beaten with a blackjack. I didn't know what a "blackjack" was when I first heard that. I Googled "blackjack," and the irony of its name and its function as an instrument of the state were sickening. She was beaten over and over again almost fatally with a piece of wood simply because she wanted to register people to vote. The police and racist state of Mississippi tried to tear the spirit of resistance away from her. They could jail her, beat her, take away her job, but they couldn't intimidate her. She once said, "I guess if I'd had any sense, I'd have been a little scared [to register to vote] but what was the point of being scared? The only thing they could do was kill me, and it kind of seemed like they'd been trying to do that a little bit at a time since I could remember." Sick of apartheid in the Magnolia State, the intrepid Fannie Lou Hamer continued to try to register blacks to vote.

It's important to remember it wasn't just the act of voting they wanted. As Bob Moses reminded us, with voting comes the enormous privilege of jury duty. Those who battled extreme prejudice saw that the ultimate honor was to be called for jury duty. The voter registration movement wanted the exclusionary stamp of disenfranchisement, keeping blacks off juries, erased, but the ink of racial hatred is difficult to eradicate. It was an attempt to upset the all-white jury system. This makes me look at jury duty as what it is, a duty rather than a burden. It is a privilege a lot of people didn't have in the country; some people were killed trying to achieve it.

"I was in jail when Medgar Evers was murdered," Mrs. Hamer said. The significance of Medgar Evers's murder so closely tied to her own arrest and beating by police officers in a Mississippi jailhouse is frightening. She knew she was almost killed that same night. She was a field officer for the Student Nonviolent Coordination Committee, just like Medgar Evers was.

She challenged President Johnson by cofounding the break-away Mississippi Freedom Democratic Party. She questioned America. She was damn right to question America. Fannie Lou Hamer reminds us, "Nobody is free until everyone is free." I was told early in my teaching career that teaching in a public school in the Bronx is a political act. Even though I get caught up in scouting reports and player development, I recognize, daily, that teaching where I teach is a hard-fought battle. Systemic inequality and institutional racism are the staunchest opponents. Within an educational world of insipid exams and mindless policies, Fannie Lou Hamer Freedom High School's stratagems run upstream from the traditional model of teaching and high-stakes testing factories. The school questioned that model and found it to be highly ineffective for a large portion of the Bronx. I have come to believe every kid deserves a great school with great teachers with great coaches and great teams. I also believe in the concept found in the Mishnah, *tikkun olam:* any effort to try to repair the world is good because the world is broken. That's what Mrs. Hamer wanted to do. *Fannie Who?*

That's "Fannie Who."

SEVEN TO GO

We clinched our playoff berth way back in December. We had seven games left in the regular season. Seven stages before the playoffs. Morrisania and Archimedes were in second and third place, respectively. Up first were reunions with Annex and Hyde, two divisional teams we'd met in December. As with all reunions, people change. We were a different team since the loss to South Bronx Prep. We offered up a bizarre impression of ourselves to the basketball gods. We won both games, but they were not pleased with us: We were losing at halftime against Annex. Tyree went 0-for-8 from three-point land against Hyde. The well was empty. The SBP loss had clearly punctured our spirit.

At each practice I wanted to cure the pain by telling them how we could beat South Bronx Prep in the playoffs, but I didn't know how. The reasons why we lost and how we might not lose again have escaped me. My mouth was full of sour grapes. I had become undone. There were things to be said to the team, but I didn't know how to say them without destroying their fragile egos, and with the playoffs around the corner I wanted to build them up, not tear them down.

Kenneth, always reliable with a bicep flex after an exciting play, looked like he needed a new go-to move. The bench celebrations weren't working. They were perfunctory at best, and meaningless at worst.

Anything I could offer would be empty words, and players know when coaches are mumbling insincerities or meaningless phraseology picked up from a soundbite from last night's NBA game. And I don't have Brad Stevens's demeanor or acumen. On the other hand, Brad Stevens doesn't coach in the Bronx. Plus, I don't think even he would have an answer to South Bronx Prep.

HAVE A GOOD PRACTICE

"Use the glass," I encourage. "It's your best friend."

Today practice starts with a shooting drill, steps from the rim, using the backboard. The backboard rests in midair, almost invisible, but an essential part of the game. The gym has an earthy smell. The heating duct blows hot air like a hair dryer as the guys take turns aiming for the perfect spot on the tempered glass.

"Serve the platter. Reach for the cookie jar. Hold your release." I impart essential shooting instructions.

Good shooters all have one thing in common: the hand that pushes the ball toward the hoop ends up resembling the Hebrew letter *Vav*. After a shot, great shooters extend their shooting hand for what seems like minutes, long after the ball has gone through the net, as if a spotlight should shine on just the shooting hand. What most people don't see is that behind every perfect shot is the off hand or the guide hand. The hand that helps the ball stay balanced. The hand that leaves the stage right before the shot is released. The guide hand is central to the success of any decent shooter.

Jessica is my guide hand.

My wife has a significant influence on my coaching and teaching. Through the highs and lows of a season, she nudges me to be consistently kind and understanding on and off court. She's the balance and support I need.

"Have a good practice" Jessica's text read before every practice.

The setting sun amplifies the translucent stains on the back-boards. Glass backboards are eternally smudged. Yet like all windows, they still work even when they are dirty. We look beyond the grime. The boys are aiming for the white square on the glass, searching for the most sacred spot, where the ball hits the glass and the net and avoids the rim altogether. I'm watching their release and where the ball hits off the glass; each shot, examined precisely for where it strikes the glass. Every shot is as distinctive as a fingerprint.

Coaching high school basketball is hard. Being married to a coach is even more difficult. Work infiltrates all marriages. My wife can measure the seriousness of a practice by the hoarseness of my voice. She experiences firsthand the jagged differences between a win and a loss. She counts the hours I am away from home, and senses when I am thinking about the game when we are home.

At times I'm too attached to the game. Too focused on an incident that may feel like vandalism but is just part of the game. I get caught up on the blemishes. Sometimes her texts are more serious: "I never have enough, enough time from you, less worry about the girls, taking care of myself, the family, never feeling I have enough to give the ones I love what I would like to. And often feeling like I don't get what I want."

Yet when I get home, she always asks how practice was. Jessica rectifies my bad moods. She improves my tunnel vision, not just for the team, but for the family. She cures myopia. She operates in perspicaciousness.

Jessica is my Windex.

She's there to remind me that it is just a game. She wipes clean the self-pity and doubt.

"Figure out what happened. Fix it. Make sure the boys are okay and get ready for tomorrow." This or something similar is said as we sit down for dinner.

"And when you are done, can you hang the new shower curtain, change Salome's diaper, check Nina's homework, fix the printer, unclog the toilet, and take out the trash?"

Jessica reminds me that it is okay to be imperfect. It is also not okay to become fixated on perfection. Teams that succeed aren't bothered by their imperfections. They embrace their strengths. Their confidence grows. And she reminds me that I am responsible for helping young men feel confident about themselves. Additionally, she points out there is also a bunch of household chores that I need to do.

Jessica is the axis on which this team rests.

One thing I have come to discover about life as a coach is that there are two essential rituals that happen around mid-January. The first brings about a certain unhappiness in the team. They have spent too much time together. Too many two-hour practices. Too many bruised egos. Too many injuries that never get a chance to fully heal. Teams and coaches have to come to terms with these facts.

The other rite of passage for any coach is the inevitable quarrel with the spouse. I swear, the shorter days of the basketball season play a serious role for basketball coaches. I wonder, do the coaches who coach a spring sport get yelled at as much? Basketball is a long season, and each season I don't spend enough time with my wife and kids.

The middle of the season is when a coach's team and personal life are at the extremes. There's a pull to stay at home and do ordinary things with the kids, like watch another episode of Elmo or go sledding or just sit and build with Legos for an hour. Jessica and I both know we need to get a babysitter and go see an off-Broadway play or a movie with subtitles. But we don't. We are usually too tired. January leaves me stranded on an emotional island: stuck between ambition and familial obligations: "But reflecting I am reminded that I am so blessed with more than enough. Each year I struggle with your connection to basketball, but at the end of the season I am always so proud of you and the boys."

I can tell when the cup of patience Jessica poured before the season started has evaporated. I am an imperfect husband. I can't pretend there is full reciprocity during the season. It's very unequal. Each year's a complete overhaul, and it's really unfair to the family. The support Jessica has given me is beyond appreciation. I rely on Jessica for balancing and edification. Jessica allows me, sometimes begrudgingly, to devote a lot of time to coaching. And I'm a coach my team can rely on because I have someone at home I can rely on.

Jessica is also my best friend.

"MY FOE OUTSTRETCHED BENEATH THE TREE"

When we walked in, all I saw were rules! Lots and lots of rules posted everywhere! After a few minutes, I expected to see some type of five-year plan or a warning against tomfoolery or you'd be sent to the gulag public school down the street where all the inmates, like the crew of the *Pequod,* were made up of "mongrel renegades, castaways, and cannibals." We were in the lobby of the decadent Uncommon Charter School franchise. The information desk was not unlike the one at your local hospital or law firm, except this one had a litany of school safety agents who easily could have been mistaken for local gendarmes. We were instructed that food or beverages would not be permitted, but we could buy drinks and food in the gym. The charter school heist is for real.

By now most folks are aware of the well-meaning charter school plan to bring flawless education to the inner city. Under the banner of choice, they empower parents to have a say in their child's education. But deeper underneath the banner of choice, charter schools are tightening the noose around struggling public schools. Charter schools have swapped out the underperforming students, the special education students, and students with behavioral issues with the docile and the ultra-motivated. Their motto is: "Work Hard. Go to College. Change the World!" Or rather: "Work Hard. Be Nice."

The noise coming from charter schools tends to obscure rather than clarify their intent. They want us to think they are providing an excellent education, and they might be. But at what cost?

This is what is known as the "paradox of the positive." In a paper written by the educators Robert Heath and Damion Waymer, they suggest that these grandiose claims usually marginalize populations and promote exclusion. How can we allow the most marginalized and excluded people in this country to be squeezed even more?

A specter is haunting the urban public school system. It's dressed up like a public school, it takes public money, yet it is exempt from the rules, very important rules that the rest of schools play by. Charter schools have cast off the fraternity urban public schools have had with each other. Tacitly, if not willingly, we have agreed to have missing lights in our bandbox gyms, where teams wear uniforms that are faded, or worse, where the colors have run into each other to form a unique color combination. We have agreed to take *all* students. Charter schools don't.

The charter school boom is an opportunity for profit. It's replete with financial incentives. We should be troubled by the success of charter school expansion because it robs neighborhood schools of many resources. We are witnessing the birth of a charter school industrial complex. It is unclear what the future holds for them in New York City, but at present, one thing is clear: they have now increased their sphere of influence to include producing top basketball teams. The only way I can fight this menace is by beating their basketball teams.

The top eighteen teams in the B classification were invited to play at the annual Class B Showcase on the last Saturday in January. Here the PSAL officials could get their eyes on teams throughout the city and help accomplish the herculean task of seeding sixty teams for the citywide playoffs in February. We were scheduled to play Democracy Prep, the Harlem-based charter school. The games were hosted at the Uncommon Charter School, the larger and richer uncle of the charter high schools in New York City. This was the second year in a row the PSAL had scheduled us to play a charter school at another charter school. Last year we played Uncommon Charter School at the Knowledge Is Power Program (KIPP) in the Bronx.

In the years since charter schools entered the PSAL, they have performed exceptionally well on the court. Last year for the grand finale, KIPP, the McDonald's of the charter schools franchise, won the PSAL basketball championship. The story could have been a small progressive public school slays a corporate charter school in the finals, but that wasn't to be, since we lost in the semifinals.

We entered the gym. "Yo, Fannie Lou, you guys play upstairs!" a handsome, bald black man in a yellow bow tie and blue shirt yelled out. The Uncommon Charter School gym, was, well, uncommon. It was the Taj Mahal of basketball courts: three full courts on the second floor.

"Upstairs?" I asked. We were trying to catch our collective breath.

"Yeah, on the fourth floor," he directed.

We walked up the stairs and entered an exact replica of the one on the second floor: three more full courts, and of course all the lights were working.

New York City is an extremely unequal and segregated city. Asking us to come to a lavishly appointed charter school was insensitive at best. And playing a charter school inside another charter school was like sailing by Scylla and Charybdis while fighting with the Cyclops in the saltbox. It was double indemnity.

I rely a lot on poetry and literature to navigate experience. I don't know any other way. A moment like this sent me running to William Blake's "A Poison Tree":

In the morning glad I see
My foe outstretched beneath the tree.

Charter schools may soon dominate the PSAL. Brand-new coaches. Brand-new buildings. Donors with hands in their padded pockets patting themselves on the back. They laugh at our ancient interiors and shabby exteriors. The PR department of the charter school complex publishes articles by the dozen about the bravery and sacrifice of all those on board charter schools, not so subtly hinting that the teachers at the public schools may not be as smart or as brave or as good-looking as theirs are.

We were escorted to a classroom to change. It was complete with a view of the Manhattan skyline, and was more Ikea than Bed-Stuy, where the Uncommon High School is located. The school reminded me of Switzerland with black and brown people. I can see classroom rules everywhere. Rules for grammar. Rules for life. No-excuse pedagogy reigns. I was trying to get ready for the game, but I had too many questions. How can the plebeian public schools compete? How do charter schools teach resistance when they want everyone to act the same? So many important movements in history are about informed dissent; this place looked like it wanted blind obedience.

I changed into my Chinese New Year Kobes for this game. This was not vanity. This was coaching. I couldn't match the school's facilities, so I let the team focus on my sneakers. I wished they'd notice my Dražen Petrović shirt too, but alas they didn't. The sneakers were enough to release the pressure of the game and to distract them from the immaculate surroundings. I can't rock Armani suits like Pat Riley did, but it's the same idea: when your coach is fresh, everything else is fly.

"Ooohh, Coach, when did you get those?" Josh asked.

"Fire," Tyree said. "Pure fire."

It's all about peacocking at the right moment to relax the team before a big game. They got dressed and prepared to face the best B team in Manhattan, the Democracy Prep Dragons. The team we were warned about before the Maspeth game a month ago. (In my mind I kept thinking that I wanted to open up a school called Socialism Prep.) The coach of the Dragons was Dominic Fanelli. He had a telegenic Midwestern smile, like a weatherman who promises and delivers sunshine every day.

He said, "I like your warm-up."

"Thanks," I said curtly.

On this particular day it did look good. The ball was sharply thrown, heels were off the floor on the pivots, hands were ready for the catch, the cuts were timed perfectly, the passes on target. I looked at the armada and right away saw that the Dragons were missing their center, Alihassane Soumahoro. Coach Fanelli was searching my face for sympathy. I could see he was nervous.

The older of the refs blew his fearsome whistle to start the game. Shamar's cheek was cobwebbed with toothpaste, and a little sleep caked around his right eye. Time to wake up. There were ten scoreboards around the gym. They all worked. The game started off the way a bus leaves the Kiev bus station in January: slowly. Tyree's hair was growing back, and he seemed to be getting his stroke back with it. He hit three threes in the second quarter. At halftime, we were winning 26–15. On the way to the classroom, we walked by plaques recognizing students' achievements and where they were going to college.

"Coach, we should have something like this at our school," Walfri said.

"I'd like to see a list of all the kids they kicked out of here," I replied.

We were playing our trademark defense that day, and Democracy Prep was locked out of the paint. They started settling for three-pointers, some of them launched from the Apollo Theatre back in Harlem. On the other hand, Shamar kept getting layups against them, and by the end of the third it was 42–28. We eventually won 66–34. Tyree finished the game with 19 points. Charles had another double-double, 21 points and 10 rebounds. Shamar was once again brilliant, with 10 assists and 15 points.

South Bronx Prep played Adams Street after us and won easily. The dust was settling: it looked like they would be the number-one seed and we would be the number-two seed. That meant the only way we could meet again was in the championship game.

A SECOND CHANCE

We piled inside the van. Our victorious white omnibus drove us back to the Bronx. Playoff seeds were on my mind. It was January, but it felt like February. The season was coming to a close. A year ago, my daughter Salome was jiggling around inside Jessica. Now she was almost walking. Soon she would be a one-year-old. The team had also grown up a lot in a year. Without the bus, Uncommon High School would have been impossible for us to get to. I was very thankful for having a supportive administration. I couldn't have become a good coach without a strong administration behind me. First Nancy Mann and now the new principal, Jeff Palladino. I was lucky to have supportive principals. Gaby always says, "Takes teamwork for the dream to work." He was right.

We arrived back to the Bronx faster than expected. We hopped off the bus, and the team huddled around me on the sidewalk next to the school.

"Great game," I said.

Twilight was falling.

"Hey, what's going on here?"

An NYPD police car had driven up on the curb. Two policemen jumped out and shielded themselves behind the open doors.

"Just a coach talking to his team, Officers," I said.

"Okay," they replied in unison. The cops pulled away.

"That was crazy!" Charles said.

"It was like magic. You waved your hand and they went away," Bryant said.

"They didn't even ask us if we won," I replied.

"Imagine what would have happened if Coach wasn't here?" Frankie asked.

At this point everybody used Mohammed, the freshman cameraman, to demonstrate their experience with police. They feigned headlocks, arm bars, frisks, choke holds, curb kisses, and wall hugs, mimicking encounters—real or imagined, it didn't matter. After everyone had exhausted their police experiences, we went home; some up Jennings Street, some to the 4 train, the rest down West Farms Road, all of them still shaking their heads at what just happened. The next few days we talked about white privilege. Incidents like this allow us—force us—to talk about race, poverty, privilege, and justice.

In the cab home we passed by Timmy Hariston's building. Timmy graduated in 2016 and was off playing college basketball at Corning Community College. Since freshman year, Timmy had buried himself in basketball to escape his difficult life. He played center; at six feet eight inches tall and 290 pounds, his job was to take up space, which he did very well. He gathered rebounds when they found his hands, and by senior year he was a crucial part of our run to the final four. One of the highlights of his senior season was Timmy making his first and only three-point shot of his career. After the shot he moonwalked back on defense, licking his hands and then like a sharpshooter in a Western putting them back into his imaginary holster. It was one of the funniest moments of my coaching career.

Timmy's size was intimidating to tiny guards flying into the paint, and it also was a problem for some police officers. In the summer of 2014, the same summer Eric Garner was choked to death by an overly aggressive police officer in Staten Island, Timmy was also brought down by several policemen in a stop-and-frisk gone wrong, and a choke hold eventually made him relent. I was happy he was in college and sent him a text.

"How's the season going?" I typed.

I missed him. I end up missing all the guys who play for me. I also worry about them after they leave Fannie Lou. We spend a lot of time and effort to help children transform their lives, but poverty has the power to undo a lot of the work we accomplish. I feel it's important to try to keep in touch with everyone, even after they graduate. What would have happened if I wasn't there? Would the team have been arrested? I don't know.

FRANKIE'S RETURN

"It's dumb cold," Bryant said, his large red headphones keeping his neck warm like an ermine scarf.

"I told y'all it was mad brick," Shamar said.

We stood frozen, waiting for the bus. The vapor of our warm breath clouded the Bx11 bus windows when it finally came. But wouldn't you know it, we would still have to walk a half mile in the cold to get to Morrisania High School, past the frozen carpet of leaves and the puddles of ice. Our extremities will have given up and the blood will retreat. Not a testicle will be descended. One of the biggest drawbacks of away games is the commute. New York City public school varsity teams use the train and the bus. There are no yellow buses to bring us to the games. Once or twice a season, the school can procure us a white omnibus for away games. The rest of the time we use public transportation. Can you imagine trying to squeeze a basketball team onto an already packed subway car with tired commuters at rush hour? It is an act of magic.

Here we are in the heart of winter. It has been several days since I have had direct sunlight. We got off the Bx11 bus and made our way across the sylvan Crotona Park. The hills were blanketed in hoarfrost. The smell of the Chinese restaurant over on Third Avenue made me hungry. Once we get into the

school, we passed the mercurial school safety agents and quickly
changed in the locker room. Often it's a bathroom stall, where
the guys rotate in like a dressing room at Macy's. Here we do
our best; we walk long distances in the cold to our games and
we don't have a proper place to change or store our belongings.
We put our bags behind our bench. I start to think back to the
conditions at the charter schools.

Here at Morrisania High School, you walk into the gym and
the lights are fading like the four o'clock sun. The crowd doesn't
dare take off their jackets. It might be warmer outside than it is
in here. The ancient gyms of New York City are small; they are
from a different era, contradicting everything we teach about
basketball. We want spacing on offense, but there is no room to
move when the top of the key touches the circle at half-court.

"Tonight, I want you to pretend we are playing half-court.
There are no fast breaks in this gym," I said.

Over the last few years, I have applied the famous lines from
Dante's *Inferno* to this gym. It should read, "Abandon all hope,
ye who enter here" above the entrance. Morrisania's is the small-
est gym in the PSAL. It has the dimensions of a Porta potty. Of
course Morrisania was undefeated at home this year, because
everyone plays like crap here. Our bench and their bench almost
meet at half-court, separated only by the scorer's table. At the
table were three oversize teenagers. The refs looked like they
were also worn-out from the long season. One ref is fighting
ennui and losing. The other is so intent on this game getting
over as quickly as possible, he leaves his earrings in. Over the
years, I have gotten to know these guys pretty well, and I knew
this was going to be a quick game. A 4:30 p.m. start and a
5:30 p.m. finish, maybe six whistles, and they would cut the
halftime minutes from a ten-minute break to five. That might
not be so bad, because tonight was Salome's first birthday and I
wanted to get home for some cake and ice cream.

"Coach, where is the bathroom?" Bryant asked.

"Down the hall to the left," I answered.

Somebody had to pee. Somebody always has to pee. The gym was filling up. Space was limited, and yet more and more fans arrived. They sat on the floor opposite the bench, their warm backs up against the cold cement wall. There I spotted Frankie's mom. I waved and walked over to hug her.

"You know, Coach, I couldn't come to the games and see him on the bench. It broke my heart," Caridad said.

"That's two broken hearts," I confessed.

"Well, good luck, and thank you for all you do for my son."

Coaches across the country shudder at the phrase "parental involvement." I welcomed it. Sigmund Freud said, "A man who has been the indisputable favorite of his mother keeps for life the feeling of conqueror, the confidence of success which often induces real success." I needed all the help I could get, and Frankie's mom, while absent a large part of the season, was here tonight with bottles of Gatorade for the whole team. Tonight was Frankie's first game back since breaking his foot, ironically playing the very same team he broke his foot against in December. He had been practicing, but we planned to play him only a little in the second and fourth quarter.

A few days before he was medically cleared, he asked me, "Coach, so how's this going to go?"

"How does what go?"

"Me coming back and stuff," Frankie said.

"Did Tom Brady come off the bench when he came back?" I asked.

"I don't know," Frankie said.

"Never mind, you are going to let me know how your foot feels. Your lungs and legs will burn too," I warned.

He was worried about the team's chemistry. We were 19-1. I wasn't worried at all about the team's chemistry, because Frankie's the best teammate of all time. I was worried that he would move like a starfish while everyone else moved like barracudas.

The game begins and we can't move. Morrisania can't move. The beautiful game of basketball was not meant to be played within these dimensions. It was claustrophobic at best, and at worst it felt like it would be a better idea to play three-on-three. Here we are in a tar pit game on a frozen night in January struggling in Morrisania's inferno. This is what dinosaurs must have felt like after the asteroid hit. It may not be the end of the world, but this game feels like it. I see the two basketball teams and I don't recognize what they are doing. Suddenly I realize I have seen this type of game before. It looked like Miami Heat versus the Knicks circa 1998. Ultra-physical, plodding; I thought this type of basketball had been outlawed when Jeff Van Gundy was used as a broom at Madison Square Garden.

When Frankie entered the game, he looked and moved like Han Solo after he was removed from carbonite. Unsteady. He was out of tune, like dusty piano strings. Yet this was the perfect game to slowly get his feet wet. Not one of those greyhound games we played against Smith or Comprehension Model School earlier in the year, which would have been too much for him.

Before the game, we reminded the guys over and over to play the game the best they could despite the conditions. It was great to have Frankie back with us. It was the same feeling I had when my daughters' grandparents came to visit. Someone is going to sweep the floor after dinner, someone can help do the dishes. I wasn't expecting a lot from Frankie, but a little bit of housecleaning goes a long way.

We traded the lead all game long, and the horn sounded with the teams tied at 64. The Morrisania players celebrated at half-court. It was the surreal moment of the season: the game was headed to overtime, yet they were acting like they had won a championship. I had to look at the scoreboard multiple times. I asked the refs what was going on and they didn't know. They'd thought they were going to get home quickly. Ulysses S. Grant begins his memoir this way: "Man proposes, God disposes."

We won 77–66 in overtime. Frankie was 4-for-4 from the free-throw line in the extra period. He ended the game with 7 points. His comrades did what they had been doing all season. Charles had another monster game, 20 points and 20 rebounds. Walfri and Ty had double-doubles too. While those four guys played well, I saw Shamar looking over his shoulder too many times. Tonight would be JB's last start, effectively ending his season. Mack's minutes would also shrink now. They were all worried about Frankie's return.

FEDERALISTS

Frankie had come back, and the potential for a bad chemical reaction was now becoming more obvious. He was going to take playing time away from guys. He was going to take shots. We also knew he was going to add things to the team. Teams, regardless of an injured player's return, have a tendency to implode toward the end of the season. This interval between the regular season and the playoffs is usually when the pull of the season goes slack. In order to minimize unforeseen mischief and maximize our chances of not losing in the first round or the second or ever, I needed to do something. Most of the time we scrimmaged other teams. I hate scrimmages. I was preoccupied with finding something else to do. Something creative. Something new. Something exciting.

"Marc, you guys want to scrimmage this week?" A text from Chris, the Clinton coach, arrived.

"My place or yours?" I asked.

In a lot of ways, teams evolve like the United States. The transition from the Revolution to the failure of the Articles of Confederation to the genius and stability of the Constitution wasn't easy. A few years ago I was selected for a James Madison Fellowship. One of the requirements was to attend its summer institute. The James Madison Summer Institute lasts six weeks and is held at Georgetown University: the same grounds where Patrick Ewing blossomed, John Thompson fought Proposition 48, and the Georgetown president sold 272 slaves to resolve some old debts in 1838. One of the requirements for the fellowship was an essay on the Constitution. As a basketball coach, I tackled the *Federalist Papers* with a particular interest: "Madison clearly envisaged the imbroglios that would ensue during ratification. He agreed with Hamilton that safety was paramount. To secure safety, he wrote *Federalist #10*, suggesting some remedies against the fear of a monolithic society." I was not satisfied with this essay. I sat up late every night, reading Madison and Hamilton, thinking about getting in shape, and writing fragments about the 2014 San Antonio Spurs. What I really wanted to write was a treatise on how to prevent my team from killing each other before the playoffs started. Madison and Hamilton seemed like the perfect candidates to study. A New Yorker and a Virginian wouldn't make great teammates, but they had agreed on a common goal: a constitution.

While coaches traffic in preparation and avoiding losing, players enter the playoffs with uninsulated bravado about winning. Who doesn't prefer the glory of the latter to the sadness of the former? This part of the season makes me want to jump out a window: From February 10, we would have to wait until March 2 to play in the first round of the playoffs. That's twenty days without a game. Each February we also get a week off from school. That's five days without school. February eats my soul.

Everything we worked toward gets unraveled in February.

The rhythm of the game fades, practices are less intense, and the season stops. Over vacation those vital sleep patterns are disturbed. The structure of school evaporates; it's difficult to be late for a three p.m. practice after school, but it's likely that 75 percent of the team will be late for an eleven a.m. practice on a Wednesday during the inaptly named Winter Vacation. We needed this time to improve in a few areas. Frankie's injury had a dual effect: the team now knew we could win against most teams without him, but we needed him to beat SBP. Some fractures don't heal in a cast.

The deceleration of basketball invites distractions. Miraculously, this season we sidestepped the girlfriend insurgency or siren call, the call of duty to babysit younger siblings, drugs, evictions, suspensions, arrests. Of course, girlfriends become more important as the season draws closer to an end. The sirens call, or more likely they text. Twenty days off and there were numerous ways to "disturb the tranquillity" of the season. I didn't want to lose our dexterity, finesse, endurance, timing, grit, strength, or hunger. I was helpless not to.

When pushed to come up with ideas of what to do over this break, we set up fake games called scrimmages. Clinton became one of three scheduled scrimmages. The guys have limited patience with these delusional activities. Ideally, the scrimmages work and we get to run our offense against another team's defense, stay in gamelike shape, and break the monotony of playing against each other in practice. On occasion, there can be an ego bubble that bursts.

For example, against Clinton, Charles came off a dribble handoff and launched a three-pointer.

"Can you take one dribble and attack the rim, please?" I begged.

Charles paused. Obviously upset and embarrassed, he walked off the court and sat at the end of the bench. He thinks that I think he can't shoot. Here there is an issue of communication and trust. I probably should have explained for the twentieth time this season that his jump shot is not statistically sound. This was our first confrontation in three years. Yet I seemed to have one like this every year. Last year it was with Rory Brown.

I remember it well. "We can't double-team if you're not playing defense!" I yelled at him. I was already hoarse in the first quarter. Rory's shoulders dropped, his eyes closed, and his jaw muscles flexed. On the next possession, Rory dribbled off his foot. Then, back on defense, he didn't even bother to rebound. I was forced to sub Rory out early in the game. Sometimes, removing a player from a game can be like dancing with a rabid wolverine.

"If you're not going to rebound or play defense," I told him, "you can watch from the bench."

"I'll watch from the bench and we'll lose," he threatened.

We're both about to start screaming insults at each other. Simultaneously, I considered this a direct challenge and understood that he was trying to assert his perceived importance to the team.

"No, we won't," I retort. "We will not lose this game. Watch."

At that moment, Rory took off his jersey and walked out of the gym. Why? How? It was clear the disquiet of adult life had penetrated into his adolescent world. How many kids have wanted to quit because someone was asking them to rebound? The finality of taking off your high school jersey for the final time shouldn't happen in public. It should be a sacred moment with your teammates. This isn't supposed to happen, I thought to myself. Not Rory. He was a four-year player. One of the best defenders I have ever coached, who emptied his tank every game.

Rory said good-bye to his youth, to his dreams, and begrudgingly walked out of the gym and into adulthood—his cocoon of high school basketball ripped open. When I entered the empty locker room after the game that night, I found his discarded shorts and sneakers scattered across the floor, as though he busted through his chrysalis too early. Why did Rory quit? I hadn't seen anything coming at all, and Rory's unprecedented departure that night left me and the team thunderstruck.

Was Charles going to quit too?

I was so attuned to how the players were treating each other, I lost focus on how I needed to interact with them. Charles's angry reaction wasn't the only thing that felt like last season. For the second year in a row, we finished 23-1. The absence of actual games allowed Frankie's return to produce an aura of jealousy, and rivalries percolated underneath each pass and shot. Practices were chippy and more intense. Now a dark cloud of potential quitting reemerged on the horizon. If Charles went, I might lose a lot more of this crew. As the days went by, practices lost their intensity and spontaneity. Like Ahab, I wondered, "The short and long of it is, men, will ye spit fire or not?" What would we do in the playoffs? Quit? Forget our roles? Misplace our desire?

I returned to the Hamilton and Madison playbook. At the Summer Institute, there were some forty high school teachers. Together, between lectures on Madison and visits to Montpelier, his plantation, I would sneak off to the gym and bump into old Georgetown greats like Dikembe Mutombo or Othello Harrington. I should have asked them about jealous teammates and irascible coaches.

At the end of the Summer Institute, I figured out how Madison and Hamilton worked brilliantly together to produce the *Federalist Papers*. They would break up soon afterward. I was enthralled. This idea of people working closely together and splitting up later once the common enemy was vanquished was brilliant. The days before the playoffs were plenty, as were the distractions. I could create the common enemy—me—but I wasn't sure that was sound practice.

That evening I went to the gym and watched the Washington

Wizard and former Georgetown guard Otto Porter shoot what must have been a googolplex of jump shots. In between water breaks I read Hamilton: "Men are ambitious, vindictive and rapacious," he writes in *Federalist #6*. Well, so are teenage boys. We all harbor those "private passions"—like the ones where a guy thinks he deserves more playing time than another guy. I walked back to the dorms past the magnolia trees. Their scent was as unfamiliar to me as the song about Shenandoah everyone in class seemed to know.

How can we survive these twenty days? Each day would be an iteration of *Federalist #6*: "revolt . . . menacing disturbance . . . rebellion . . . discord . . . hostility . . . aggrandized themselves at the expense of their neighbors." Left alone, the team will make war on each other, or on me. I know other teams were experiencing the same thing. In *Federalist #7* Hamilton "suggests that the motto of any country opposed to the United States should be *divide et impera* [divide and conquer]"; this became a useful strategy for us to employ before we cannibalized each other.

This team had the benefit of a deep playoff run last year. But I kept seeing a thread of smoke that I imagined was a hidden blaze behind the door. A fire I wouldn't be able to put out. For the whole twenty days, I suffered manic thoughts tackled by delirium, nightmares of missed free throws, disorientation, shoulder cramps, cold sores, night sweats, back pain, visions of Charles following in Rory's footsteps, strep throat, athlete's foot on my itchy right toe, joint stiffness, loss of appetite. My stomach felt like it was tied into an ancient sailor's knot.

Alams Beato, our statistician, was also Charles's best friend. He acted like a modern-day Patroclus, best friend of Achilles. I asked him to talk to Charles and put a salve on our relationship so we could make up and go into the playoffs ready to do battle. Alams came to the rescue. I'm not sure what Alams said to Charles, but it worked.

GOGOL IN THE BRONX

In early February, another polar vortex has invaded New York City. In Washington Heights, the icy wind darts off the Hudson River while Nina and I walk up the street to the bus stop. It feels as if the wind has teeth and is biting my ears. Either Nina's pants have shrunk or she grew an inch overnight. There is a space between her pants and socks about the size of a coffee cup. Her shins are pink from the cold.

"I had to walk to school when it was colder than this in Moldova," I said. "Then when I got to school there wouldn't be any heat."

"Is Russia colder than Moldova?" Nina asked.

"Yes," I said.

I open the weather app and show Nina my phone. For some unexplainable reason I added the city of Yakutsk years ago to the list of cities on my weather app. I have never been to Yakutsk, but the coldest city on earth has always fascinated me.

"Today Yakutsk is minus-twenty degrees. They also have lots of diamonds there," I said.

"Does the ice make the diamonds?" Nina asked. "I think diamonds need warmth to be shiny."

Here's a potential deep dive into negative numbers, geography, and my strange obsession with Russia, but it is too early for a math lesson, too cold for geography, and there's not enough time to talk about Russia as the yellow school bus is impatiently waiting for us.

Today is the first day of the spring semester. Like on all first days of class, making an impression is important. I kiss Nina good-bye. I pedal faster to school than on most days. I'm excited. In the next few months I will get to teach my favorite subject,

Russian literature. We will spend time with Tolstoy, Babel, Pushkin, and Gogol. Unfortunately, we will run out of time before we can examine Dostoevsky. When basketball ends, this class helps me stay afloat. I can honestly say no other body of literature comes closer to capturing the misery and joys of coaching basketball than Russian literature.

How can Russian literature be akin to coaching high school basketball? There exists an undeniable if invisible thread binding basketball coaches with the starting five of Russia's greatest characters: Tolstoy's Anna Karenina, Goncharov's Oblomov, Dostoevsky's Raskolnikov, Pushkin's Onegin, and Turgenev's Bazarov. Gogol's Akaky Akakievich and the Brothers Karamazov can come off the bench to man the second unit. Are all great basketball teams alike? Is each bad team unhappy in its own way? Who knows? What I do know is a winning team has somehow solved its most vital problems: toxic egos, inefficient shot selection, foul trouble, lack of size or speed. In truth, all happy teams are different; each one solved a specific problem to avoid losing. Clearly, all losing teams are the same: they failed to win. The concept of sacrifice is essentially a Russian tradition. When you win a championship, slights over playing time are forgiven. Those verbal transgressions, a rite of passage in the realm of the athlete-coach relationship, are washed away by the tide of winning, and the season becomes a positive experiment in brotherly bonding. When you lose, no one escapes innocently. A loss can turn you into a paranoid Raskolnikov.

To young coaches I say: beware of the Anna Karenina principle. When I first started coaching, I couldn't handle losing. I was prone to overreact after every loss. I felt like throwing myself before the next oncoming train. Soon you realize losing sucks, but it is not a deep despair. We all lose. It's not that I got used to losing; I still go out of my way to avoid losing. But it's a simple, irrefutable fact that you are going to lose games, and coaching basketball may make you the happiest guy in school one day and other days make you miserable.

There's a special pleasure teaching Russian literature. It is the chance to watch and listen to children talk, write, and think about the largest country in the world. A place that also occupies a suspicious corner of our American collective consciousness. When reading Gogol's *The Overcoat,* students read about an experience that is not unfamiliar; a man dreamed of a fancy jacket that he couldn't really afford. He was then robbed of that fancy jacket. Who wouldn't want to get revenge on that person? Akaky Akakievich, the main character, is able to haunt the bureaucrats who did him in. It's the ultimate revenge ghost story.

The Bronx is very far—geographically, politically, and culturally—from Russia, but today the heating system is down and my classroom feels like Siberia. All we needed were some big furry hats and a Vladimir Vysotsky song to complete the setting. The longer I coach the more I see coaching as a parallel to the Russian novel; the subplots, the minor characters, the obstinate players, the paroxysm-producing plays, the unforgettable games. The subplots give the season their unequivocal vitality. The great plays and players become stories for the next generation of Fannie Lou Panthers.

The regular season is over and the playoffs start March 2. For a brief time, I can concentrate just on my classes. In a few weeks the gospel of team ball will be put into practice. For the time being, I am messianic about Tolstoy's *Hadji Murat.*

"There's a story about a man walking through a field of grass. Imagine the field has been plowed. And he comes across a lone blade of grass that somehow survived the blade of the tractor," I say, opening the discussion. "It takes strength and a little luck to avoid the guillotine of life."

Retelling *Hadji Murat* in the Bronx on a freezing February

morning didn't really do it justice. Tolstoy wrote, "Man has
conquered everything and destroyed millions of plants, yet this
one won't submit." It's a lesson about Chechnya's relation with
Russia. It's a lesson about empire. It's a lesson about durability
and luck. Bryant and Kenneth are the only guys on the team I
teach this semester. I will use it as a parable with the team: we
want to be that plant that will not surrender, that one team that
is left standing at the end of the season. Students see themselves
as the blade of grass, the one person in their family to graduate
high school and go to college. Teaching Russian literature and
coaching basketball provide me with wood on the fire. I find
whenever I am exhausted, Russia helps me. Hearing Russian on
the streets, going to Tatiana's restaurant in Brighton Beach, or
watching my favorite Russian film, Andrey Zvyagintsev's *The
Return,* are like an ennobling salve.

I tell the class about the time I went to the Russian sauna
in the East Village. There I witnessed an abnormally pliable
Tajik wrestle with an old friend of mine. The Tajik whipped
him with birch branches and then folded him like a pair of
pants. Uncomfortable, I left my friend and slipped into the
ice-cold pool. Here, surrounded by barrel-chested men, their
nipples half submerged in the icy bath, I could only stare at the
water. This idiosyncratic process of exposing yourself to extreme
temperatures is supposed to allow you to experience epiphanies.
I like to think it was in the icy pool, corralled by men twice my
size, that I realized coaching basketball is like a Russian novel.

I let the students know early that Russian novels are famous
for the multiple names their multiple characters possess. In
Russia, patronymics are vital. The books mirror real life. There
are two or three different Nastashas in the same story—just
as you might know three different Jacks in your life. Gogol
and Tolstoy both overpopulate their novels, and we are left
confused as to who the main character is, or if the information
is important. Yet this happens all the time in life.

"Noah called."

"Which Noah?"

"Not sure."

In Russia it would be "Vanya Ivanovich called." No questions need to be asked. Vanya, the son of Ivan. That Vanya.

Every class is built on the process of forming some type of fidelity in the children to reading, thinking, and writing. In the classroom or on the court, literature allows us to see our own personal awkwardness and inconsistencies. Or it mitigates a loss. Or gives meaning to unexplainable events.

A friend once asked, "Do your students really like Russian literature?"

Every year I hear either "Kids these days are impossible" or "I've never had a better group of kids." That's teaching, right? And coaching? And life. Life comes at us in waves. Sometimes we are sailing, other times sinking. In the end I can never forget I am working with someone's child. The passive and slothful Oblomov reminds a journalist, "Don't forget that there is a human being there. Where is your humanness? . . . Love him, remember yourself in him and treat him as you would yourself—then I will read you and bow my head before you. Give me a human being, a human being!" These are not fictional characters in my class, but real kids, with their own as-yet-unrealized dreams unfolding before us. Do they like Russian literature? They love it.

Over this season, I have seen Shamar and Walfri morph into very good basketball players and perform admirably in the classroom too. The X's and O's of the season will fade. As will the plot twists and dialogue of this class. A coach's passion or a teacher's enthusiasm melts away the coldness of the unfamiliar. What remains is the human connection; a relationship that rests on trust. In the end it doesn't matter if I was teaching students how to play the digeridoo. The ever-present sense of devotion in a teacher evokes both an awakening and a feeling of pride in students. It all comes down to an infectious element. Students become owners of their learning. I have watched this unfold over and over.

You'll find coaching basketball or teaching Russian literature is not so unlike your own life. There's a rhythm to the season that's filled with the duality of the unpredictability of games and repetitiveness of practice. Russian literature has a mysterious universality that makes the logorrheic student listen and allows the silent student to say something profound. Students don't want super lesson plans with lots of gizmos and gadgets. They can see through transparent actions. Lesson plans don't win students over. Teenagers aren't impressed with intellectuals. Knowing this and acknowledging it are important. They like adults who treat them with respect and dignity.

Like a fireplace that takes a while to heat a cold room, students warm up over the semester to strange names and alien backdrops. Throughout the semester the students have various reactions to the stories we read. When we meet Tolstoy, Michelle E., an eleventh grader, sees the kindness and contradictions of the Russian soldier held prisoner in the Caucasus. Leaving the mountains for the city, we encounter Gogol's St. Petersburg, where Anthony G. relates to Akaky's temptation to buy a fancy coat. Wislady asks about how societal pressure shapes us and forces us to buy stuff we don't necessarily need. Diamond describes the pain of loss, even if it is a coat, and the ache it can cause. She suggests there may be justice only in the afterlife.

We continue to Pushkin and Babel. Bryant observes how characters lost their moral fortitude, like Herman in Pushkin's *Queen of Spades* and the soldier in Babel's *My First Goose*. I watched Sebastiann excitedly compare Herman's desire to unlock the secret in *The Queen of Spades* with Akaky's obsession to retrieve his jacket, and how it led them both to ruin. He sees ambition as a vice; a warning in life. Zayasha pronounces that we have to experience something to know it. As she is getting ready for college, she is infatuated with how the characters' identity shifts through these short stories as her own identity is shifting before us. There's a beauty to reading and teaching here. The fateful collision of the Bronx meeting St. Petersburg through Gogol and Pushkin and experiencing the surreal beauty of Tolstoy's Caucasus makes me smile and generates a little warmth in the freezing classroom.

HARPOON

I was home alone. Jess took the girls to Maryland for the weekend. The goal was twofold: she could spend time with her best friend, and I could spend some time writing this book and subsequently get ready for the playoffs. I planned to create a basketball bunker. I wasn't leaving until I figured out a way to get this team ready and devised a way to beat South Bronx Prep. I would order takeout. I wouldn't leave my desk. I would watch coaching clinic videos and read endless articles looking for the right word or phrase that would shift the rudder toward a championship. I would spend hours in my self-imposed basketball prison watching games: Fannie Lou basketball, the Filipino national team, Celtics, Warriors, teams from upstate New York, anything I could find on YouTube. Charles was right, it was hunting season.

As we were preparing for the playoffs, President Trump announced he would ban CNN, the *Los Angeles Times*, the *New York Times*, *Politico*, and the BBC from the White House briefing. I was taking notes on the new tyranny unfolding in America. Was I being tyrannical? To play for me, you have to abandon the five-dribble move. You have to have faith in statistically sound shots. We want wide-open threes, free throws, and layups. Finally, I was able to conceptualize the postseason with an easy-to-remember alternative axiom, all with the letter *P*. I called it "the three P's": Pace, Pressure, and comPosure.

I can remember the practice we found out the seedings. We would play Robert F. Wagner High School.

"We will play Wagner on Thursday," I wrote on the whiteboard. With twelve wins and four losses in the season, Wagner was going to be a formidable matchup. There are a lot of great coaches in the PSAL, along with a lot of talented players. I knew the Wagner Panthers would come in ready, and it was my job to get my team prepared.

Practice began as usual. Shots. Dribbles. Three-on-two, two-on-one. A modified fast-break drill. The announcement unified us. Now we had a common opponent. The ball raced up the court. Suddenly, a loud pop resounded. Mack was down.

"Oh, Coach, this isn't good."

He was holding his leg. Later we would find out Mack had a torn patella and would miss the rest of the season. And it happened just when we looked to be a complete unit. We needed everyone on deck if we were going to go deep into the playoffs. The one thing about Mack's injury: it cleansed us of any fears or jealousy. Mack, a junior, had served honorably as the backup point guard. His injury coalesced the team. They seemed to realize the finality of the injury. Maybe his career was over. They knew the end of our season was also near. They sensed we needed even more unity and team spirit and less pettiness and selfishness. Strange that *Troilus and Cressida* would be so filled with coaching aphorisms. Shakespeare in the Park is one of the greatest gifts to New York City. I borrowed another line from the play: "Troy in our weakness stands, not in her strength." We had to eliminate our weaknesses and stop worrying about the other teams' strengths.

That night after practice, as if I hadn't overfilled my cup of basketball, a couple of friends and I went to the Lehman College–CCNY semifinal game. A great game, it ended in a buzzer beater by CCNY. My heart sank. I watched Coach Schulman, the Lehman coach, walk across the court after the loss. He looked like the loneliest man on earth. Because of games like this I am never sanguine going into the playoffs. March can be so cruel. It's about missed opportunities, injuries, bad luck. The vagaries of the game linger long after the buzzer has sounded. Sometimes you get only one shot to kill the whale.

PART THREE

PLAYOFFS

NYC HOOPS

You might be surprised to learn that New York City is the fountainhead of college basketball; we have everything from Michelin-rated hoops to fried chicken spot games. It's an all-you-can-eat buffet. In fact, even most New Yorkers don't know there is more college basketball in New York City than any other city in the world. College basketball is something of an afterthought on our sports menu, but in fact you could feast on it in New York City throughout the winter.

For example, the table is set on any given Tuesday. Dress in layers, because the gyms are hot and the streets are freezing. In January you could attend the battle of the Jesuits: the Manhattan-Fordham game in Riverdale. Get there early; the pews are filled quickly by hungry Fenians. Then you can head south into Manhattan on the 1 train to 181st Street. Grab a sesame chicken on a *laffa* at Golan Heights. Walk by the Dominican teenagers rolling blunts on Amsterdam Avenue and watch the kosher Fighting Maccabees of Yeshiva University battle the College of Staten Island Dolphins. Reminder: don't forget your Blistex, the winter wind will burn your lips. Jump on the M101 bus to City College and visit the home of the iconic coach Nat Holman, "Mr. Basketball," and the site of the 1951 basketball scandal that shook the world of amateur athletics. Next, stroll down Broadway to Levien Gym for some Ivy League basketball: the Columbia-Harvard game. (You'll need reservations.) If there are too many screens and each team is sycophantically overpassing and being overcoached, we can leave.

Then I suggest we hop on the Metro-North to New Rochelle for dessert. The highest-scoring offense in the country is thirty-five minutes away at Iona College; you won't be disappointed. There's Division II basketball at Queens College, and more Division III at Baruch College around the corner from the world's number-one restaurant, Eleven Madison Park. I haven't even mentioned the bounty of Brooklyn basketball yet. The motherland of Connie Hawkins, Bob Cousy, Chris Mullin, Bernard King, Billy Cunningham, Roger Brown, Dwayne "Pearl" Washington and *tutti quanti,* up to Stephon Marbury and Lance Stephenson. If you still have some time, there is the junior college circuit. Hop over to the Boogie Down and catch the Hostos Caimans and the Bronx Community College Broncos. I'm sure this game isn't on anyone's bucket list, but it's a heated rivalry nonetheless. While in the Bronx you must try to taste-test the artful Apex Center on the Lehman College campus and see the Lehman Lightning versus the John Jay Bulldogs. New Yorkers love basketball as much as their restaurants. There is plenty to eat and see. It is hoop heaven for the epicureans.

In the summer Pro City, Rucker, Inwood, Dyckman, West Fourth, Watson, and Gersh leagues take over the playgrounds. However, the real prize of New York City is not college hoops or the summer blacktop games, but high school basketball. The colossal talent of the Catholic League, the whiteness and privilege of the Independent League (read: private schools), and the hoi polloi of the Public Schools Athletic League.

In the old days before the collapse of the Mecca of basketball, before the YouTube sensations, before traffic cones were defenders, before dime-store AAU teams, in those days when centers were central and point guards were prophets of the asphalt, when the scholarship players were plentiful, when players played in the park because that was where the competition was, when everyone was a Knicks fan because they competed, when everyone hated the Chicago Bulls for ruining Ewing's dynasty, coaches enjoyed respect in the city because they were seen as defenders or saviors, keeping kids off the streets. Then a few of them went to jail for molesting kids. Basketball's holy reverence in New York City was crushed by the misdeeds of a few false legends.

The game shifted away from experienced coaches teaching the game and moved to anyone with a whistle around their neck. Basketball requires learning and coaching, along with the idea of teamwork and discipline. There was a total shift from people who knew the game to people who thought they knew the game. This democratization of coaching has pioneered a whole new style of basketball and the sort of player who plays it; one who is concerned only about how he plays, not whether his team wins or loses.

When I first arrived here, it was intoxicating just to be in New York City. Basketball players from across the world know the parks, the courts, the players, the coaches, the legends. In 1988, a grainy VHS tape of Kenny Anderson somehow made it to New Hampshire, and it was the greatest thing I had ever seen. He was undeniably unguardable. Nobody could stop him. He moved like hand sanitizer. He just killed defenders.

In New York City, the appreciation of the dribble is something akin to worship or a civic duty, like standing for the national anthem. When somebody is about to work someone, the crowd rises, phones quickly become cameras waiting to capture the poor victim. The crowd laughs and smiles; it is unadulterated schadenfreude on the blacktop. Spectators bask in the glow of the awkward defender's imbalance or the poor dude whose shot was just pasted off the backboard.

Before I was a coach, there was a disconnection between the city and me. I would get this strange feeling walking into a gym. I remember I would walk by Lou Carnesecca or Jack Curran and think they looked familiar, just not sure how I knew them. When I became a coach I would be chastised for not recognizing

Lloyd Daniels in the corner, or Tom Konchalski and his yellow legal pad perched in the stands. I felt the same way walking the streets of Jerusalem. I didn't know that I was walking one of the Stations of the Cross until a horde of tourists almost trampled me. I was too embarrassed to ask where to find King David's tomb. The history can be overwhelming.

And that's just it. Every gate in Jerusalem has stories. Every gym in New York City has stories. I remember coaching a pre-season game at the Gauchos Gym in the Bronx, genuflecting on the hardwood, drinking tap water from the same pipes that quenched the thirsts of Jamal Mashburn and Ed Pinckney. New York City has a mystique like Jerusalem; there's no other city like it. Glass backboards stand in for the religious iconography. Gyms serve as our temples and cathedrals. Pilgrims are the fanatics. The keen appreciation of basketball and food in New York City is as real as worship. Every New Yorker is either a food critic or a basketball fan. There are few ascetics in the city. Most imbibe either the hardwood or the neighborhood Indian joint. Some of us partake of both.

THE GRAND ARMADA

The PSAL Class B playoffs have grown pharaonic in size with the growth of small high schools throughout the city. To qualify for the playoffs, a team just needs to be at .500. This year fifty-seven teams made the playoffs. As with any tournament this size, it is a winner's world. Lose and you are out, done, finished.

I stood in the middle of the court with Gaby and Kyheem during practice. We've created this panopticon where we can see everything: charting missed layups and unresolved bad habits—Charles keeps lifting his pivot foot before he dribbles. Cris's left thumb pushed the ball and produced this strange elliptical spin. Tyree was not low enough on his cuts, he needed to push off the inside leg. Kaleb avoided attacking the basketball and moved east–west instead of north–south. Frankie dribbled two basketballs in concert up and down the court, staring at his sneakers instead of looking ahead. All their basketball sins were confessed before us, and their transgressions washed away in fountains of sweat. Their practice jerseys were stiff as a priest's collar with seasoned perspiration. Months of hard work, eighty-something practices, and all I could surmise was . . . "We need to organize our feet."

The next day in practice, we worked on simply catching the ball, pivoting, and passing. No grand strategies. No giant overhaul. No remodeling. Simple footwork drills.

I have this haunting premonition or fear that if we lose tomorrow, that means today was our last practice of the season. That means Walfri and Shamar's last time practicing with their high school team.

Tonight didn't feel like it was going to be our last practice of the season. It was March and the playoffs finally started tomorrow. I thought of a line from the Russian poet Osip Mandelstam: "A thick fog swirls in front of me, and behind me there's an empty cage." The regular season was behind us. There is the certain uncertainty of the playoffs waiting for us. More questions to answer: How would we play after all this time off? Did the time off help Frankie's foot mend? Will the time off mess with Ty's timing? Is Charles exhausted? One thing was clear. Walfri's and Shamar's careers would end soon. Just how soon we didn't know.

WAGNER

When the Robert F. Wagner Panthers finally entered the Fannie Lou gym, I was feverish. "This is going to be my flu game tonight," I told Gaby.

Wagner was led by their coach, a young man in khaki cargo shorts. I was worn down. The last few sleepless nights, combined with biking in the cold and eating poorly, had done me in. Nina helped me get dressed this morning. She picked a blue tie with small orange, yellow, and red fish on it for me to wear. "The fishies will make you feel better, Daddy," she said.

Coach Andrew Pultz walked over to me and Gaby. I looked past him, as I was trying to examine the young men who looked like trees that followed him.

"They are huge," I said.

A massif of teenagers started to warm up. Two players were around six-eight, and another looked to be around six-five. Inches of opposing players are magnified in our little gym.

"I told you." Gaby had scouted them in Queens.

"Hey, Coach! Great season," the Wagner coach said.

As if our season was to end tonight. It smelled of false civility and had a hint that he wanted to upset us. We had been waiting twenty days to play, and I felt dizzy. What am I supposed to say after this encounter? I could say, *Yeah, and if you beat us tonight it will be the worst night of my life.*

"Thank you," I replied.

"I heard you also have a new baby at home," the Wagner coach said. This is the oldest trick in the book: disarm the opposing coach with dad talk.

"Well, they are over there in the stands." I pointed to my family.

I couldn't do this. I couldn't put up a fake front of civility with harmless chitchat. Coach Pultz was firmly planted in the catalog of young coaches who balance family and work. He coached girls' volleyball in the fall, basketball in the winter. While he was trying to disarm me, I watched his team warming up. They wore pine green T-shirts that read "No Gym—No Problem."

I admired them for embracing their spartan success without a home court, but it wasn't like Fannie Lou had it made. I was being cold to Coach Pultz as the fever wreaked havoc on me. I guess it's just who I am. I drag my feet on paperwork, I swear too much, and I have a difficult time turning the sarcasm spigot off. Before games I really don't want to talk to the other coach. Doesn't he know I want to drink his blood?

"Let's Go Panthers!" The crowd was already into the game. They too had been waiting almost three weeks for basketball.

From the start it was clear Wagner wouldn't be able to handle our pressure. In the end, no matter what else, New York City basketball is a guard's game. Frankie and Shamar were tandem thieves robbing the Wagner guards of everything they owned. It wasn't only that they had a difficult time getting the ball over half-court. It was as if nobody wanted to try to break the press. And when they did, their moderately talented big men were no match for the much smaller Charles and Walfri. In the second quarter, I sat there feverishly, watching in admiration as Charles coiled up like a snake and pounced on the two big men, drowning their hope of an upset with a two-handed dunk plus the foul. This was his trademark: a dunk that simply deflates teams.

What happened before the dunk may have looked ordinary to the casual observer, but it was actually another trademark of Fannie Lou basketball. Frankie passed to Shamar at the top of the key. Shamar ball-faked. This was an indicator to set Walfri and Tyree in motion from the opposite sides. Walfri and Tyree ran by each other. We know teams come in trying to defend Tyree three-pointers, so movement on his part usually causes a lot of attention from the defense. This is what coaches call gravity. He pulls the defense closer to him, and that leaves other players with more space to attack. Walfri screened the middle of the zone. Shamar whipped the ball back to Frankie as the defense shifted to Tyree. Frankie found a wide-open Charles, who had enough space to wind up and dunk it.

Above all else, my team always impresses me because at their age they know ball movement is paramount. We hadn't played in twenty days, yet our discipline, timing, and passion were all on display. It was 28–15 at the end of the first half. As we walked to Room 103, Nina ran up and handed me a bag of cough drops. I grabbed a handful.

"We need a run to bury them. In the playoffs you cannot keep teams around. There are way too many things that can happen." I paused and unwrapped a cough drop. The cherry cough drops rescued me. My voice was faltering.

"Keep the pressure on and push the ball."

Now in the playoffs, we started a new Latin chapter: *Divide et impera*. Divide and conquer. In the third quarter we went on a 15–0 run to bury them. We won 65–38. After the game Nina ran up to me.

"Momma was cheering for the other team," Nina said.

"Jess?" I asked.

"She kept cheering, 'Let's Go Panthers!'"

Mascot duality is a fact of life in New York City. There just aren't enough animals to fill the halls of all the schools without some overlap.

"I didn't know they were also the Panthers," Jessica confessed. "Who do you play next?"

Behind every good coach is a great wife. None of the success I have had on the court would be possible without Jessica.

TOWNSEND HARRIS

Next up was another school from Queens, this time the elite Townsend Harris Hawks, the eighteenth seed. Within the New York City public high school system are specialized schools for each borough: The Bronx has Bronx Science High School. Manhattan has Stuyvesant. Brooklyn has Brooklyn Tech. Staten Island has Staten Island Technical High School. And Queens has Townsend Harris. The Hawks had already beat two Bronx teams, Grace Dodge and Bronx School of Law, Government and Justice High School. Townsend Harris was led by Jonathan Mea, a talented lefty point guard, Andi Rustani, a six-three sharpshooter, and their leading scorer and rebounder, Justin Miller. Justin was a small mountain of a young man. He had 33 points and 23 rebounds in their win over Bronx Law.

This would be our final home game; after this round the playoffs move to a neutral site. I fished in my pocket for a cough drop as I looked over at the Hawks coach. He held a desultory, crumpled piece of paper close to his nose, maybe a scouting report or a printout of our stats. He was bowing ever so slightly at the hips, and his lips were moving like he was quoting midrash. He was trying to figure out who we were when we knew everything about them. Coach Bitis from Maspeth gave us film. He knew he didn't have a chance. I didn't disturb his prayers.

I gave some last-minute instructions: "Force the point guard to use his right hand."

"Walfri, do not help off number thirty-five. Just lean on Justin all night. No space."

It was 25–6 at the end of the first quarter. We won 82–48.

This was our most Soviet performance. Walfri delivered like a

Stakhanovite: he held Justin Miller to 16 points and 12 rebounds. We had five guys in double digits in scoring, led by Shamar with 23. Nothing can stop an egalitarian offense. Frankie had a career-high 10 rebounds. Charles was once again unbelievable, with 18 rebounds.

THE GREAT TRANSITION

In 2012, I found myself wondering if coaching could get more painful than this: My team and I stood stunned. Some fans were arguing time had expired before the last shot, but the refs ignored them and briskly left the gym. In front of us, the young men from NEST+m, a gifted and talented high school on the Lower East Side of Manhattan, were celebrating their improbable last-second playoff victory, a half-court buzzer beater. If every loss is shattering, this one was unforgettable. I always felt I could keep coaching after a loss. I was pliable. Unbreakable. Until now.

I left the gym thinking this was my last game. I was broken. A cloud of unrequited hopelessness hung in the gym. I couldn't deal with the pain, and neither could my team. My team had the kind of apathy you'd find in a Buffalo Bills locker room. We had collapsed. These early playoff games owned me. Despite our stellar regular-season efforts, we were missing something in March; something mysterious.

My first six seasons we won more than we lost. In fact, in 2012 we won twenty-five games, a school record. We had a margin of victory somewhere around thirty points a game. We weren't just winning, we were *destroying* teams. We possessed an unshakable faith during the regular season that somehow came undone easily during the playoffs. Did we press too much? Did we peak too early? The narrative had shifted. Winning in the regular season was no longer an achievement; it was starting to resemble pre-failure. Here was another late-season catastrophe after an admirable regular season.

Before the game I thought I was a good coach. After the game I knew I wasn't good enough.

When I got home after the loss, I left the duffel bag full of wet jerseys in a corner. I didn't feel like washing them. I didn't feel like doing much of anything. Then Nina, who was almost three years old, hugged my leg.

"Daddy?" Nina asked. "Can you read me a book?"

"Of course," I mustered.

The season was over. I was devastated. Yet what little girl has time for adult disappointment? Nina pulled *The Little Red Lighthouse and the Great Gray Bridge* off the shelf. If you are a parent, you know that, as with any favorite bedtime books, your mind can wander as you're reading the words both you and your child have memorized. Nonetheless, I love rereading. Especially this book, because I can see the George Washington Bridge from my apartment.

Even writing about the view feels like sharing a family secret. I know if I ever move I will never again have a view like this. It is like a portrait on the wall changing before me. The seasons change: chunks of floating ice in February contrasted with the greenness of June is surpassed only by the foliage in the Palisades across the river in New Jersey in the fall. When I look out the window, the little red house remains just out of sight.

"Daddy," Nina asked. "What's your favorite book?

When I first read *Moby-Dick* I was traveling in Uzbekistan, unmarried and restless. I thought it was all about a young man and his adventure. When I reread it years later, I thought it was about the pursuit of something unattainable. The last time I reread *Moby-Dick,* married and domesticated, it felt like spiritual coaching instructions. Sometimes I'm Ahab. Sometimes I think I am Ishmael. I have never thought I was the whale until tonight.

Was coaching more like Ahab's blind obsession than Ishmael's ability to navigate total ruin? We are all Melville's Ahab in pursuit. We are all Melville's whale when we are harassed. We may try to avoid a conflict, but force us into a corner or hit us with a harpoon, and we are likely to send your crew into the depths. We are all Melville's Ishmael: observing, listening, composing a narrative, hoping to survive to tell the tale. *Moby-Dick* is still a powerful guiding force in my life. After a loss like this is when we confront our own Ahab. The one who lives in us.

I coach for personal reasons. I coach for societal reasons. I coach to live. If I tell you that I want to coach for personal reasons—the wins, the banners, the trophies—I come off as vain. If I tell you about the societal reasons, you may think that at best I am naive, or at worst I am morally superior. When I admit that I coach to live, I want you to think of a coach as you would a painter or a writer. Someone who works on their craft and extracts pain and pleasure from the process. Coaching is about precisely that. It is an art.

I now know that in my first six years of coaching, the conditions were unripe. I think we needed time to implement and bring everything into alignment. There were two freshmen on the 2010 team, Michael Castillo and Jimeek Conyers, and they witnessed firsthand how a talented bunch of seniors who didn't share the ball, took bad shots, and blamed each other for defensive mistakes would always fail in the playoffs. At the time, I didn't know the central art to coaching was controlling the passion. The ego is such a powerful force. Feed it too much and it becomes fat and lazy. Ignore it and it fades away. But it never dies. When I tried to deconstruct my first years of coaching, I encountered a lot of resistance. It was because I didn't embrace everyone all the time. Our egos were not balanced. If the game is equally distributed, then come playoff time the pressure of the game doesn't fall on the shoulders of one or two players; the pressure needs to be equally distributed throughout the players on the floor throughout the season. The same way tension is spread throughout a bridge. A bridge to a better team.

Basketball allowed me to trust adults again. That my trust in the universe was sometimes broken didn't matter on the court. Coaching allowed me to reestablish trust with young men who may have had the same issues with adult trust that I had. Truth lives in the space between a player and coach. The hours spent in the gym allow different conversations between a coach and his players. I started to see coaching like the Great Gray Bridge: a chance to build something trustworthy. A chance to build something kids could depend on. Nobody walks over a bridge they don't trust. A bridge to a better version of ourselves. Yet these playoff losses were weakening the bridge.

There was an absurdity in expending all my emotions on this sport, on the season, on this game. I was depleted.

The target was winning. It never moved. I was a good coach, but far from great. Minor calibrations didn't work. New plays were fruitless. New players weren't as committed as the older guys, leaving us in a position of never quite being a varsity team; always three juniors and four seniors. Maybe it was time for a junior varsity team, I thought. How could we make the leap? Increase practice intensity? I'm fairly intense, so I don't think that was it. My coaching philosophy of team ball versus hero ball wasn't going to attract the most talented individual players. The championship formula seemed unsolvable.

Being driven by the same feeling of being semi-competent each year is dizzying. Anthropologists call this the liminal space or liminality. To be more precise, I lived on the threshold of meaningful coaching. Coaching makes me feel my life is important and has meaning. Art does this too. It was the same mechanism. I coach because I wanted to be recognized as someone who could coach. I knew my X's and O's. Still, something was missing.

The familiarity of our season ending before the playoffs did, not dissimilar to reading a book over and over again, felt like I was building a bridge to nowhere. In *The Little Red Lighthouse and the Great Gray Bridge,* the forgotten lighthouse becomes the hero of the story. A children's book was the embodiment of the season and my career. The idealistic approach to coaching was to coach with your heart, coach them unconditionally, and win a championship in the meantime. In theory this was a solution to the passion trap that shows up every March. Like a mad captain who knows that without hunting for the whale, you'll never find out what it feels like to kill the whale.

Obviously, I didn't quit. The following season, Jimeek Conyers and Michael Castillo, now seniors, willed the team to the school's first PSAL championship. Michael and Jimeek grew up with Dean Oliver's Four Factors. Our practices and film sessions were fortified with basketball analysis: offensive rebound rates, effective field-goal percentage, turnover rate, and how many times we were able to shoot free throws. We eliminated all mid-range shots. We strictly shot three-pointers and layups. By this time Mike was an undersize power forward with the heart of a lion, and Jimeek a water bug of a point guard with the armor of a rhino. We added Corey Morgan, an athletic center, and a few three-point specialists: Kenny Bonaparte, Tony Crespo, Oscar Norales, and Isaiah Thomas. We were well on our way to the top of the pyramid among small high schools in New York.

With data applied to basketball, I now had a weapon of math destruction. But the championship in 2013 wasn't won just with analytics. Numbers don't protect you from the emotions of teenagers, or poverty, or the vagaries of the game. In coaching you are always waiting for the unexpected shoe to drop, unfortunately, you are waiting for Chekhov's gun to go off. When will the mercurial forward quit? Who will be injured? Suspended? Who will have a cold shooting night?

I started to bring Nina to Sunday practices for two reasons: I love the feel of how a basketball team works, and I thought she could see our partnership in action; and out of necessity— Jessica worked the weekend shift at the hospital. I thought it was important for Nina to see how hard the guys worked in this little shoebox of a gym. Nothing fancy going on here. Just old-fashioned teamwork.

Nina has never asked me why I'm so devoted to this team or the school. She just knows that when she comes to practice she gets to play with the iPad. Nina is unaware of which player lives in a shelter, or which player didn't eat breakfast because he didn't have any food in his house. She doesn't know about the young man who limps because he has fragments of a bullet in his knee. She doesn't know about the player who has SAT flashcards in his backpack. She can't see his dreams of being the first person in his family to go to college. She doesn't know whose brother is locked up. She doesn't know that not one kid in the gym, including me, actually grew up with his biological father. She has no idea of the number of unrelenting demands on the players. They think it's funny she won't even pick up a ball to dribble. She gives some players high fives, and with one or two she's unnecessarily coy. I have always thought she needed to see where her father spends a lot of his time, with young men who love this game and depend on me to help them become better versions of themselves. Her world consists of eating a cheese stick on the bleachers with an iPad on her lap at this moment. A little girl with her glowing iPad helped me cut through the fog of coaching.

The beam of light from the iPad, like a lighthouse, glows in the gym. Unknowingly, she was helping guide me to become a better coach. You have to enlighten as a coach, not build a bridge on hope alone. Help your team understand the complexities of life. When they ask why a certain school in the suburbs has an athletic trainer and an ice machine, the conversation moves into how public schools are funded. They need adult answers to teenage questions. Nina became the fuel to become a great coach because I wanted her to be proud of her dad. Nina helped me embrace the imperfections of my team. We all have them. She taught me that a committed coach should grasp his team's dysfunction and their incompleteness as children, as students, and as players. The same way a husband loves his wife or a father loves his daughters. If deep inside we know we have our own dysfunctions and weaknesses, then by truly understanding my team's blemishes I could help them shine.

Nina became my lighthouse. When I started embracing our difficulties and not trying to hammer them straight, she helped me see that those rough playoff games were unsuccessful because stress was not distributed throughout the team. Assistant coaches had a duty to perform; the last guy on the bench, the shot clock operator, the managers all had jobs to do. In all sports you need to win in the playoffs to legitimize the program, and everyone needs to perform well in their duties.

I was focused on building a bridge and I forgot I needed a lighthouse. Rereading a book I had read dozens of times to my daughter on the worst night of my coaching career helped me realize what my coaching needed: light. I asked Nina why she likes *The Little Red Lighthouse and the Great Gray Bridge* so much, hoping to add more insight to coaching, fatherhood, and life.

"Because," she said. "It is right there." Pointing outside the window to the illuminated George Washington Bridge. I didn't have to swivel my head. She was right. What was missing, in two words, was a lighthouse.

QUARTERFINALS

On to the quarterfinals and back to Uncommon High School in Brooklyn. We were scheduled to play my friend Mike King's team, the number-ten-seeded Community Health Academy, located in Washington Heights.

"They love to shoot the three," Kyheem said. "They have this one kid whose release is unreal."

"They play the Modern Game," I said.

The Modern Game is where threes are shot more than twos. Hasn't three always been more than two? The Ancients believed the closer to the hoop, the better. Pass, even force the ball into the paint was how the game was played for a very long time. Times have changed. Think about this for a minute: In 1991, at the age of thirty-four, Larry Bird averaged 3.3 three-point shot attempts a game. In 2016, Stephen Curry attempted 11.2 three-pointers a game. The Phoenix of Community Health Academy were burning up the nets. They were averaging 76 points a game and making almost fourteen threes a game.

I wrote our postseason shibboleths on the board: PACE, PRESSURE, AND COMPOSURE.

"This is the best shooting team in the city. They have five guys who can shoot the three.

"We have to defend the three." Then I repeated the words I had written on the chalkboard as we boarded the bus. (This time, once again, we had a bus.)

We couldn't get out of the Bronx. Traffic snailed and the lights were uncooperative. A quiet hush fell behind me. I intended to let the team sleep the whole way to Brooklyn. After some foolishness, they did.

When we finally arrived in Brooklyn an hour and a half later, I heard a conversation behind me.

"They are Amish," someone said.

"You mean Jewish?" someone corrected.

On the way to Uncommon for the quarterfinals was an ocean of furry sable hats parading around on the Sabbath.

In our pregame ritual, guys ran to the deli up the block for their meals of chop cheese sandwiches, chips, and Gatorade, each with his own soundtrack of Drake or Lil Uzi bumping in his headphones.

Right before games I would often listen to Bloc Party's song "The Price of Gas," about consumption, innocence, an election, and an imminent war in a fossil-fuel-rich country. The song begins with a syncopated drumbeat that reminds me of a crowd clapping in unison, the way they do in Moscow after the ballet. Kele Okereke sings, with the confidence of a farmer predicting rain, "I can tell you how this ends. We're going to win this." This became the soundtrack of our season.

It was our second time here, but Uncommon High School hadn't lost its luster. It reminded me of the Hermitage Museum. Each time I am there, I discover something I had never seen before. This time the classrooms still had the Manhattan skyline in view, but the whiteboards seemed whiter, a thermostat on the wall newer, rugs on the floor more luxurious. There were also items that I didn't inventory before: a prayer rug from Central Asia, graffiti-free desks, organized bookshelves. The money available to charter schools was well on display.

"Why don't we have desks like this?" Bryant asked.

"I'm going to tell Jeff [our principal] about this place," Walfri said.

Directions were on the blackboard: RUN THEM OFF THE THREE-POINT LINE. CHARLES AND WALFRI WILL TAKE CARE OF THE REST.

—

The first half was an all-you-can-eat sushi platter of three-pointers. It was not the Phoenix, but the Panthers who caught fire. Shamar and Tyree couldn't miss. Against Townsend Harris, Tyree's shooting had been frigid, like the polar vortex that engulfed the city that week. Tonight both he and Shamar hit rhythm threes. Shamar picked up a steal, quickly took a dribble to set his eyes on the rim, and without hesitating hit a three from deep. Right before halftime Frankie joined in on the fun. He pump-faked, took a dribble into the primeval mid-range area, and nailed a beautiful, classic pull-up jumper as the clock expired. Even the Ancients would have loved it. Frankie's bone was healed, and we were becoming something manifold and unstoppable right before my eyes. We were up 50–27. Watching us share the ball, hit threes, and play defense was like eating homemade *khinkali*, Georgian dumplings, and drinking endless *cha-cha*, Georgian brandy, with close friends on New Year's Eve. It will alter your existence. This team was becoming historical.

When we returned to the court for the second half, we waited to see what type of adjustments the Phoenix would make. They stayed in their 3–2 zone defense.

During a time-out in the third quarter, I was kneeling when I saw that Frankie's compression pants had a rip and his knee was bleeding. We threw a Band-Aid on it. He's patched up now like a punctured bicycle tire, but he had regained his legs, shooting form, and confidence, giving us a "trio of lancers": three shooters on the perimeter. We hit thirteen threes; Shamar and Ty hit four apiece, Frankie added two more, Walfri, Jaelen, and Kenneth added one apiece. Tyree was a virtuoso, with 21 points. Should I worry that Charles had only 9 points and 6 rebounds and a technical foul? No. My friend Lauren, an ethnomusicologist, once described Chopin's left hand as the orchestra and his right hand as the vocalist. Tonight Frankie played like Chopin. He had 26 points on 11-for-13 shooting, 10 rebounds, 6 assists, and zero turnovers. Sweetest music.

THE ADAMS CHRONICLES

I was still suffering flashbacks from last season. We had to play at Uncommon again. For the second year in a row we faced a familiar-sounding foe in the semifinals. Last year it was Jane Addams; this year it was the number-three seed from Brooklyn, Adams Street High School. Same gym, same seed, same situation. Interestingly, we had met the Eagles last year in the first round and Frankie hit Charles for a winning layup in a buzzer-beating out-of-bounds play. We liked the play so much we named it "Adams Street."

We continued to share counterintelligence. Coach Bitis from Maspeth sent me her game against Adams Street. Coach Ben Newman, from Lab Museum United High School, sent me his game. Adams Street had knocked Ben, a close friend, out of the playoffs, so it was personal.

Brian Shea, in his second year at Adams Street, had proven himself to be a good young coach. Jessica commented that he reminded her of me ten years ago. Young, ambitious, and squeezing wins out of a team without a whole lot of raw talent.

I didn't have the early success that Coach Shea has had. I didn't make my first final four until my seventh year coaching. Our conquest of New York City basketball had started with watching lots and lots of game film. Until recently, it seemed impossible for us to win a city title. But once we won in 2013, it became something I knew we could do again, even though a few years of playoff disappointment had filled me with some doubt.

Film creates accountability. It forces us to face our mistakes, because I'm also guilty of egregious errors on the court: substituting for the wrong reasons, calling plays for guys who weren't even on the court, not knowing how many fouls Walfri had. We must look in the mirror at our imperfections.

Every film session is a lesson in truth, but we also make sure we appreciate the beautiful things we do. We love the perfect extra pass, the precise footwork of a physical box-out, the extraordinary effort of a helping defender. If you want things to happen again, they need to be rewarded—a new backpack, a T-shirt, more playing time, a clip on social media. Film allows all of us to improve, and it also allows me to feed the monster of the teenage ego.

I secured another grainy low-fi video of an Adams Street game in December. It felt more like a piece of samizdat than a game. In vain we watch the smuggled clips for insights. The numbers on the players' jerseys are not visible. The names on the roster and their stats do not match up. Sometimes in getting ready for games like these, we just have to improvise. We can hear them yelling their offensive plays as "uptown" and "Brooklyn," two offensive plays we will strategize to disrupt. On defense Adams Street likes to put all their players on the same side of the court. They form a wall in front of the basket.

I learned about the oblique method of attack and how it worked for Frederick the Great during the Seven Years' War. Professor Warner Schilling was a luminary on the history of war. During his class, like in most of my years in graduate school, my mind would drift toward basketball.

While studying tactics and plans in Professor Schilling's "Weapons, Strategy, and War" course at Columbia, I wondered what would have happened if someone tried to beat Napoleon by using Napoleon's technique. Every so often now I get the similar urge to run the other team's play against them. Or even run a play named after the school. The Adams Street coach had mistakenly posted all his games on YouTube. I stayed up late the night before watching their last six games. They were hard to scout. This was going to be a difficult game.

In the first quarter, the matchup had the making of a conservative game of chess. Neither team could really pull away. Adams Street was up by one. Then in the second quarter we went on a 22–4 run to more or less put the game out of reach for the Eagles.

With three minutes remaining in the third quarter, we were winning 42–29. All season Charles had been tenacious and ferocious, yet he was always the quietest kid on the court. He speaks in church-like hushed tones while thunderously pursuing every missed shot. At this point in the game, Adams Street tried to play some mind games—as our lead grew, so did the trash talking. They talked a lot and Charles listened. During a time-out I heard the guys complain.

"Coach, they are talking wild out there," Charles said.

"What are they saying?" I asked.

It didn't matter. This was the moment I had happily anticipated: "Run Adams Street." Walfri took the inbounds. Cris and Shamar, simultaneously as planned, ran to half-court, while Frankie cut to the baseline, caught the ball, and lofted up a soft pass just in front of the rim. Charles then drove to the hoop and caught the ball in midair for an easy layup. On the next possession we reproduced the same play perfectly with the same result.

A nonplussed Frankie dribbled out the clock. It was a feeling we didn't get to enjoy at the semis last year in the same gym. He paused, looking at the scoreboard, to gauge the score and the seconds evaporating, a look of monumental gratification on his face. We won 73–55. I remembered that January 4 game, his sad look, an abandoned puppy at the end of the bench. Alone, listening to music to dull the pain of not playing.

The author Pat Conroy wrote in *My Losing Season* that "Sports books are always about winning because winning is far more pleasurable and exhilarating to read about than losing . . . Loss is a fiercer, more uncompromising teacher, coldhearted but clear-eyed in its understanding that life is more dilemma than game, and more trial than free pass." I agree with the first part of his statement—there's no better teacher than a loss—but we didn't have a free pass; we had had plenty of trials and dilemmas.

Here the season was ending. I took a page out of Richard Nixon's playbook. He had two Apollo 11 landing speeches prepared, depending on the success or failure of the mission. I wrote down memories from the last seven months: Tyree fouling the shooter at Clinton; Kaleb getting his only point with a little help from the referee; Charles's innumerable dunks; Frankie's valiant comeback; Shamar's unprecedented improvement; Joshua's rehabilitation in the classroom to gain his academic eligibility; Cris's proof that good things happen to people who work hard and have patience; Walfri's unmeasurable leadership; Jaelen's toughness, playing injured most of the season; Kenneth's métier, supporting his teammates unconditionally; Gaby's faith in the system; Kyheem's loyalty; Mack's fight to get back on the court; Bryant's transformation from a novice into a dependable role player; the guys behind the scene, Dalen, Mohammed, and Henry, and all their work in practice and help during the games. Only one question remained: Who would be the 2017 New York City PSAL Class B champion? That would also determine which speech I gave at the end of the next game.

THE REMATCH

After the Adams Street victory, we stayed to watch South Bronx Prep play Wingate High School from Brooklyn in the other semifinal game. The game was close. I could sense none of the

Panthers wanted Wingate to win. The team wanted revenge. We beat Wingate in 2013 for the city championship; could we beat them again when the whole team wanted South Bronx Prep? I sat next to Gaby and Kyheem, impartially developing scouting reports on both teams. South Bronx Prep finally wrestled control of the game. Up five late in the game, SBP held the ball and ran a guy baseline with less than ten seconds on the clock. No second option. What happens if that doesn't work?

Bingo! That was it! There wasn't a second option. None of their plays had second options! The guy with the ball was resolved to play hero ball. He would try to create something himself. If somehow we could force them into more hero-ball tactics, they would use up all their superpowers late in the game. At least that was what I was thinking. Was it more important in a championship game to be dominant or relentless? We had to be the latter; the former was a daydream because the Cougars were older, taller, and quicker than we were. Can we will ourselves to victory? Can we just play team basketball like we have all season? We couldn't out-finesse them; they had better dexterity, strength, endurance, and nerves. They had already beaten us, but I wasn't convinced they had a stronger will.

The stage was set. We would face the only team to beat us all year. At forty-two years old, I was still under the spell of the 1986 Boston Celtics. Thirty years later the wizardry of the greatest basketball team of all time still intoxicates me. Know what really sticks with me? My hatred toward the Lakers. South Bronx Prep reminded me of eighties Showtime. The South Bronx Prep coaches had their fancy suits like Pat Riley did, and man oh man, did the Cougars put points on the board, averaging over 100 points a game. But their point totals were necessarily lower in their first four playoff games. Playoff basketball relies on execution and an ever-present sense of calmness.

I wished I could just text Larry Bird and ask, "Yo, how did you guys beat Showtime in 1984?"

I knew the only way to beat Showtime was if we were wearing the blue collar.

You could not have created a bluer-collar team than us. Shamar and Walfri had battled back from being cut from the team sophomore and freshman year, respectively. They fought through the doubts of ever being a varsity basketball player and were now starting in a championship game. Charles had lost his best friend twice, once when he was ten years old, the other time when Latrell quit early this season. Tyree's right arm was almost severed in a strange accident. Cris battled the loss of his father. Frankie had not only traveled a long, lonesome road to recovery, his confidence was now fuel for his teammates. This team had guys who were relentless. We had guys willing to do the dirty work of sweeping the gym before the game. Everyone filled up the water bottles for one another. Everyone picked up their dirty uniforms and put them in the laundry bag after the game. They played with heart on the court. And it was evident they had compassion for one another off the court.

We had two days of practice before the championship game on Saturday. We were already prepared.

At Thursday's practice we looked ready. The passes were sharp and the attitude was merciless.

"To beat the trap, you don't use your eyes." During those two days of practice, we ran a drill where we trapped Cris and had him close his eyes. "Close your eyes. Who is open?"

"I don't know. I can't see," Cris said.

"Yes, you do," I implored. "This is not Jedi training. If Frankie's man leaves him to trap you, they will rotate to Frankie. Charles needs to flash hard to the ball. He will be at the nail. Trust me."

On Friday, a day before the game, Ty and Gaby were in my room during the lunch period.

"You know what today is?" Gaby asked.

Ty quizzically stared at me.

"St. Patrick's Day," Tyree said.

"We won the city championship on this day four years ago," Gaby stated.

"Stop it. You're going to make them even more nervous," I said.

I received a text message from Jamaal Lampkin. He was always checking up on me like a concerned friend. He was in the stands when Frankie was injured in December.

"Congrats on another finals appearance . . . proud of u man," Jamaal wrote. "U ready?"

"Born ready," I wrote back.

"Lol," Jamaal replied.

On Saturday, March 18, I had had a restful night's sleep. I grabbed my phone and scrolled through Instagram. I saw Coach Campbell's post:

> Been up all night tossing and turning so focused on today's championship game. I can't fall back asleep . . . so eager and anxious; this feeling is unexplainable. When you work so hard and sacrifice so many things to get to that point; that defining moment of your hard work and dedication . . . success and triumph is all you expect in return. "You can't ReWrite What's Already Written" I'm Locked in; Can't Nobody Take This Away From Me. How Bad Do I Want To Be Successful you ask As Bad as I Want to Breathe.

That was normal chatter. But there was this from @harlems _coach_k: "It's SHOWTIME!!!"

I finished breakfast and was about to leave. Jessica was deciphering the short red cuneiform of burst capillaries on the bridge of my nose.

"Are you okay?" she asked.

"Yes," I answered. I kissed her and headed out the door.

"Didn't you forget something?" Jess said. "Can you take the trash with you?"

I walked into school around 9:30 a.m. Shamar was there. He looked as if he had been there since last night, nervously waiting for the game to start.

"You're here early," I said.

"Yeah, I wanted to leave the house before my mom started making me do chores and stuff."

"I guess your brother can help her," I said.

"He's coming to the game," Shamar said.

"Great," I said.

"He said he wished he had come to Fannie Lou," Shamar confessed.

"I hear that a lot," I said.

On the weathered chalkboard I wrote the details for the game. Clouds of chalk were still on the board from Friday's lesson; I can see details from the semifinal game watermarked into the green chalkboard. I get this strange feeling when I am writing on top of old game plans. They are like ghosts trying to escape; they cling to the corner of the board, avoiding the eraser.

The rest of the team arrived and we went over some last-minute details. "When trapped, find Rucker and pass away from him," I instruct. Everyone is seated in front of me. We have done this close to thirty times this season. They are locked in. "He leads the PSAL in scoring. I think he probably has a quadruple-double, he has to average at least ten steals a game. We need to limit the live turnovers." Those are the turnovers when the whistle doesn't blow and it's easier for them to score when our defense is not set up.

"Here is their play 'X,' the baseline out-of-bounds play." I was giving them answers they already knew. I reviewed what we went over in practice the last two days:

- #25 the Hitman. He loves to dribble and drive. He won't have any legs in the fourth.
- #33 George Foreman. Keep him off the boards. Use a pump fake around him. Get him in foul trouble early.
- #1 Roberto Duran. Limit his big plays. He will take charges.
- #2 Sugar Ray. Make sure you box him out.
- #3 Ali. When he catches baseline he is going to spin. Wall up. If he gets out, dig and get that ball.

"Like the last four games, let's control the Pace and Pressure, and keep our ComPosure," I said.

Tyree released his hair, imprisoned all night in a black do-rag, the ripple of his hair attracting all the attention in the room. "Look at them waves." Everyone was staring at Tyree's hair.

Once the commotion had subsided, Tyree said, "I couldn't sleep last night. I was throwing up."

"That makes two of us."

We grabbed the downtown 6 train to Twenty-Third Street. Baruch College was a short walk from the train station. My mind was on one thing: How were we going to stop Ty Rucker? He led the PSAL in scoring, at 37.4 a game. He was second in assists with almost 11 a game, and had 10 rebounds a game. Ty was a smaller version of Russell Westbrook. He could score from the outside and inside. If we stopped him, there was Ali, the center. Ali averaged 26 points and 16 rebounds a game. Danny and Mark, the wings, pitched in with around 10 points a game. They had four guys averaging double digits in scoring. On paper it seemed like they had a championship formula, but it was basketball alchemy. Rucker disproportionately took more shots than anyone else, and they often ran up the score. But what happens when the game slows down and there are fewer possessions and fewer opportunities to shoot? When we won the championship in 2013, we had four guys in double digits. I have always thought if you have four guys averaging double digits, that is without a doubt a championship team. There was only one way to beat them: to have five guys averaging double digits. And we had five. Team basketball versus hero ball. I have a deep conviction that team ball in this situation will win.

We are at Twenty-Third Street when I hear the subway door open. There's a man with a crazed look in his eye. He is pushing everyone out of his way and is headed straight for Walfri. This guy just bumped into a bunch of scared tourists. Walfri's not going to back down. Walfri won't let him get away with pushing him. If this guy hits Walfri, I know Charles and Cris are going to jump in. He's about two people away from Walfri when the train doors open. Walfri and I make eye contact. "Twenty-Third Street," the automated voice murmurs.

"Everybody off!" Walfri yells. A close call.

It was March and the ground was still frozen. Piles of snow and great lakes of slush parked in front of street corners. Small valleys of snow, small enough for my feet to be side by side, allowed pedestrians to exit and enter just one at a time.

We enter into the warmth of the lobby. Move effortlessly through the metal detectors and school safety officials. We recognize each other. I couldn't tell if the escalator was broken or turned off. It didn't matter. We would have to descend gingerly into the maelstrom. We spelunked into the bowels of Baruch College. We entered the gym, where the girls championship game was going on. We would have to wait.

We sit in the bleachers. Over to my right I see the championship T-shirts folded as if they were on display at a department store. Auspiciously, they are black and red: our school colors. In the middle of the table is the trophy. It's a copper basketball balancing on a block of wood. It doesn't look like much, but it is what we came here for.

"I'm not leaving this building without that trophy," I whisper to myself.

It has been seventeen days since the playoffs started. It was quite a whirlwind trip. I was quiet and lost in thought. We headed to the locker room. I wrote on the damaged clipboard. The pink dry-erase marker, the same one I have used all season, was losing its spirit. Kenneth and Kaleb stirred uneasily in the corner.

"Coach! Space Jams?" Frankie spied my sneakers.

"It's the only way I know how to beat the Monstars," I said with a shrug, referring to Michael Jordan's movie *Space Jam*. Nobody noticed my tie, a gift from my wife. I wore a skinny, dark blue tie with mini-harpooners on it. I was prepared to explain it, at length if possible, but no one asked.

"Let's go wait near the gym," I ordered. I was feeling claustrophobic.

We had started the season with the idea of *Per angusta ad augusta*. We began the playoffs with the concept of *divide et impera*. I spotted Coach Radar. We tried not to look at each other. Civility won. We made eye contact. Shook hands. He smiled and walked away. His suit was gorgeous.

We waited in the doorway impatiently while the girls championship awards ceremony wrapped up. Radar sat down on the far end of the gym. His team was dressed in their dark blue tracksuits, the coaches in their sharp dark blue suits. I just can't get over the tackiness of some coaches' basketball attire. No coach in 2017 should be wearing those sleeveless sweaters. I don't even know where they buy them. They seem to survive in the Catholic League somehow.

My daydream about basketball fashion was interrupted by an unexpected wave. A slow, deep team battle cry of "WE READY, WE READY" echoed behind me, creating a singular intimacy I was totally unaccustomed to. It bound us together, honoring the unbelievable season.

I loved it. But where did it come from? It reminded me of a line from Dante's *Inferno*: "Do not be afraid; our fate cannot be taken from us; it is a gift." We were not a battle-cry type of team. I don't like breaking routine. But this was really cool.

The PA system was buzzing with feedback. The gym sounded like we were inside an electrified conch shell. We settled into our warm-up routine. I was lost in the oceanic murmur, staring at the stands as they filled up. The South Bronx Prep crowd found their seats. I could see a few Fannie Lou students. Here come even more Cougar fans, some wearing the "Talent Wins Games. Teamwork Wins Chips" shirts. They arranged themselves in a worshipful manner, like a church choir. It looked like the A.M.E. Zion Church congregation dressed in navy blue. My pregame reverie was broken again, this time by a voice in a red shirt in a sea of navy blue shouting with gusto, "Let's Go Panthers! Let's Go Panthers!"

Eight minutes before the start of the game, Kate Belin, the venerated math teacher who works with Bob Moses, didn't even have a seat; with effrontery and poise she yelled, "Let's Go Panthers!" over and over again as she infiltrated a hostile environment. Kate, a teacher at Fannie Lou for more than a dozen years, did her Fulbright in Botswana, was a Math for America fellow, and was a Sloan Award winner. Kate has worked with the Bard Prison Initiative. She easily annexed a partition of the Cougars Nation. Teachers, students, and alumni, all wearing red and black, joined her in the small piece of space to create an autonomous Panther Province deep inside enemy territory.

More and more friends and colleagues started to arrive. I saw Aaron Broudo, my fellow history teacher. He was wearing what can only be called a fiery sweet-potato outfit, a red puffy jacket with orange jeans. Close enough to our school colors. Ryan O'Connell, my tamale partner, was there. Coach Ben from Lab, Coach Chris from Clinton, and Coach Lawanda from BCAM were all there. There were a bunch of former players in the audience: Timmy Hariston, Ken Duran, and Shateek Myrick. I spotted Xavier Rivera.

"Have a great game" read a text from Jessica.

During warm-ups, Tyree sat down next to me. Tyree had written *MMP* in Sharpie on his kicks; I ask him what it means.

"Make Momma Proud," he said.

The opening quarter, SBP tore into us. Charles goose-stepped awkwardly after he caught the ball. Travel. He kept traveling every time he caught the ball. With about five minutes to go in the first quarter, it looked like Shamar and Charles had drunk three or four espressos. Shamar was always fast, but today he was derailing himself. He threw the ball away again. Cris subbed in for him. All I could do when he came off the court was to avoid his eyes, so I gave the floor a cold, inescapable stare.

"Settle down. Take a few breaths," I suggested to Shamar. I needed to listen to my own advice.

They must have been drinking out of the same water bottle, because Cris drove into the paint and threw up a no-look shot as soon as he touched the ball. I had to get him out of there now. I substituted Cris for Shamar, Shamar for Cris, Cris for Shamar, hoping to decaffeinate them at each visit to the bench.

"Cris, do not shoot the ball again," I warned. "This is not the time to be working on your jump shot!" I screamed.

Sometimes it helps to have the true callousness of a cantankerous food critic. *The kale salad with cannellini beans has too much lemon, the feta on the lamb burger looks like toothpaste, the chocolate fondant tastes as if it was cooked in an autoclave.*

Cris's favorite player was the former Knick and current Cavs shooting guard, J. R. Smith. They shared the same predictable unpredictability.

"Play some defense, Cris," I remember hearing a sympathetic teammate in the huddle tell him. Cris was guarding Mark Morgan, the Hitman, on the left side of the perimeter. The Hitman set him up with a series of slow, pounding dribbles. He started to drive with his left and Cris mirrored him, and then the Hitman landed one, a nasty crossover that sent Cris flying almost into our bench. The crowd enjoyed the stumble more than the made jump shot.

Cris shook it off. He was unfazed. Of all the survival skills Cris possessed, his ability to play defense after the hit was most admirable. He heeded the advice of his teammates and started playing even better defense.

At the end of the first quarter, we were down 13–7. But in the second quarter, we fought back with a few orthodox uppercuts that seemed to stun them. Ali, SBP's center, picked up his third foul and inexplicably picked up a technical foul for cursing. Having four personal fouls was crippling. With Ali out we attacked them afresh. Charles had a dunk against their full-court pressure. It looked like he could fly better than he could walk.

Later in the second quarter, Rucker drove to the hoop and was raked across the face by Cris. At the foul line he told Cris to stop pinching him.

"You better stop or I'm going to beat you up," Rucker said.

"Eat me," Cris replied.

With Ali on the bench, Rucker was not only going to have to win this game alone, he was going to have to do it angry. This simple fact transformed the championship game into more of a private feud. We had their best player looking to settle a score instead of scoring buckets.

Remember when Kevin McHale clotheslined Kurt Rambis in the 1984 NBA Finals? This was like that. Cris didn't need to cantilever anyone. Nobody knew what was happening except Cris and Rucker. You have to understand that Cris makes Charles look loquacious. And Charles is stoic 99 percent of the time. I think Cris said six sentences to me all season. I spent the first three-quarters of the season begging him to practice quicker so the games might not seem as fast. And now he was playing the role of the enforcer.

At the end of the second quarter, we had the ball with about thirty-three seconds left. The shot clock was off. We would settle for the last shot of the first half. Like all pure shooters who think they are always open regardless of time, situation, or spot on the floor, Tyree inexplicably launched a twenty-seven-footer, with twenty-eight seconds on the shot clock. Frankie, as all great captains do, cleaned up the mess, and for the next twenty-five seconds dribbled east, west, north, and south. Rucker aimed to get a steal, but Frankie's poise so counterbalanced his aggression, Rucker walked away from Frankie with seven ticks on the clock. A bruising power forward relieved Rucker to guard Frankie on the baseline. He tried to dance with Frankie, who immediately saw his mistake and backed up a few steps. Wrong move. Swish. Buzzer. Halftime.

We were up 25–21, and Tyree's jump shots and Shamar's layups were not dropping. I felt good. In the stands a series of red poster boards were held up. It looked like an Olympic opening ceremony. Seven different letters spelled FRANKIE. They shook with excitement. Like any oracle worth his weight in fortunes, Frankie had his followers, his crew, his admirers, his faithful, his ensemble, his family, and his mom.

"How many possessions?" I asked. "How many missed free throws?"

"Ten!" Gaby answered the second question and not the first.

"Wow." I felt better.

We had held the highest-scoring team in the city to 21 points in a half. My halftime speech went something like this: "They are going to make a run. Let's make it a short jog, not a sprint," I said. "They will eat our mistakes for lunch. No nonsense," I warned.

You could hear the 6 train rumbling near us as we left the subterranean locker room. I don't think there was anything I could have said differently.

South Bronx Prep came out like a runaway 6 train. I think they had an 8–0 run. It felt like a 16–0 run. The relentless vortex of pressure circled around us. *How can we escape this run before this game is out of control?* I didn't want to be like Ishmael, alone in the water as all his shipmates are eaten by hungry sharks, drowned, or otherwise lost at sea.

I called a time-out. I screamed at Frankie, "I don't care how many people are here to see you or how many damned signs there are in this gym, keep your head up when you are dribbling!"

Frankie was playing well. I couldn't yell at Shamar or Tyree anymore. I rarely yell at Frankie, and he took it on to correct everyone else. He demanded that Ty, Shamar, Walfri, and Charles get to their spots on the floor faster. He was the cynosure of the moment, and there was plenty of time left to win this game.

Cris threaded a no-look pass to Charles for an easy layup. Cris wouldn't score a point in this game, but it didn't matter—he was doing the things we asked of him. The second-quarter play when he got crossed over so hard his knees buckled hadn't fazed him. I've seen lesser plays on lesser stages ruin players. His play, however perilous and unorthodox, was a great lesson of temerity and personal drive. He wanted to be on the floor. We might have been a little awkward, but you could not question the vitality of our spirit and the power of our will. We were outscored 23–13 in the third quarter and trailed 44–38 at the third buzzer. Was our will going to be enough?

Being down by six to start the final quarter wasn't even the worst news. Frankie, Tyree, and Walfri all had four fouls entering the fourth quarter. The game was clearly slipping away. Yet we kept pushing the ball, hoping for opportunities. In a strange sequence of events, Cris looked to have an open layup, but then he hit the emergency brake and skidded at the free-throw line. Panthers and Cougars rushed by him, and he found Charles on his flank for a basket plus the foul.

"Great pass, Cris!" Mack yelled from the bench.

After the game the Walton High School coach came up to me and said, "When the light-skinned kid had the contested layup and decided to jump-stop and make the pass, that was the play of the game. Every kid I know would have shot that."

"Glad he didn't," I said.

South Bronx Prep called a time-out. The coach's game plan or visual is never mapped out in one time-out, even though there are recognizable patterns. We have only sixty seconds and try to make the most of every one; sometimes a classic player-and-coach clash unfolds, or we switch defenses, or we make a substitution, and we try to offer encouragement with levity.

"Now in the fourth is when we make our free throws," I said. "Let them beat themselves with hero basketball and we will win with team basketball."

With five minutes to go and us down 47–40, Walfri reentered the game. He grabbed a rebound and threw what looked like a touchdown pass to a wide-open Shamar—only Rucker somehow intercepted it. Roberto Duran launched a three-pointer just like the one he hit in January, but this time he missed. Walfri got the next rebound and gave it to Frankie. It was our chance to run the show. The Cougars switched to man-to-man defense and we called "G-5," our pick-and-roll play for Shamar and Charles. Shamar blew by his defender. Frazier moved in to block the shot. Shamar lifted it a little too high off the glass, but Walfri played the carom perfectly. He grabbed the offensive rebound for the bucket and the foul. He missed the free throw.

South Bronx Prep seemed to panic and drove the lane without a plan and without a pass or a score.

Our next possession had six passes. Tyree came off a Shamar screen. He caught the ball, gave a slight head fake, and drove down the middle for a gorgeous teardrop. Up 49–47. Unfortunately, Tyree would foul out on the next possession on what can only be called a phantom call. Rucker would tie the game with both free throws.

South Bronx Prep refused to take the press off. Frankie got the ball and found JB wide open for a layup. He was fouled hard.

He missed the first one. And then South Bronx Prep called a time-out.

"Coach, JB keeps talking during free throws," I heard someone say as we gathered.

He had just missed three free throws in a row.

The warm huddle buzzed. I could see the crowd shifting in their seats, their eyes begging for access. I was close enough to examine the geography of their chapped lips, the pea-shaped snot pinned to Charles's cheekbone, the wing of skin falling off Frankie's knee. Ty was rubbing his right arm, the one from the accident; it had started to stiffen up a little. I needed to iron the defiant wrinkle from JB's brow. I noticed the dry-erase markers had stained my palm like wedding henna.

"Not now! JB, stop talking trash and make your free throws. This is not the time to be screwing around." His face said, *Who snitched?* Then he missed his second free throw.

On the next possession with three minutes remaining, in a tied game, Coach Radar handed his players the poison chalice of the stall. The same one we had seen against Wingate. In 1977, the legendary Dean Smith, coach for the University of North Carolina, lost a national championship game versus Marquette using the stall. Seconds ticked away and minutes remained. It was an error of judgment. With ten seconds on the shot clock, we knew a player would run the baseline, but this time he wouldn't be open. We got the stop we planned for. We got the stop we needed.

The intensity started to pick up. The ball was deflected near our bench. The ref quickly gave the ball to Walfri. He quickly got the ball to Charles. Walfri recognized nobody was guarding him and cut to the hoop, and Charles delivered a perfect give-and-go.

One minute remained and we were up by three. South Bronx Prep had the ball. In a flash Rucker drove the middle against Shamar and Cris, and the ball came loose. Walfri picked it up, and in a sequence we practice every day, the ball moved quicker than the dribble. Here lies the art of coaching: I have a strong conviction that a team that plays together will beat hero ball. And if one play could dispose of the Leviathan, this was it. The ball sped ahead to Cris. He moved it back to Walfri. Walfri found Shamar at half-court. Shamar took one dribble and saw Charles pointing to the sky. That's where Shamar threw the ball. Charles found the ball floating in the air and ferociously threw the ball back toward earth with two hands. The indelible dunk. Anyone who saw it will never forget it.

In the iconography of *The Indelible Dunk,* the quietest kid had the loudest, most iconic play of the season, of my coaching career. He was up in the heavens wrestling with angels. On his return to earth Charles let out a vengeful scream. Gaby and the crew jumped out of their seats. It was the play of the game, of the season, of our lives. The dunk disabused not just the Fannie Lou fans but anyone in the gym of any notion that we weren't going to win: the refs knew it, the crowd knew it, Ms. Jackson, our beloved school safety agent, knew it. The dunk was the fatal blow. The harpoon to end the hunting season. The whale was dead.

In essence, the game was over. We were up five with forty-five seconds to go. South Bronx Prep immediately called a time-out. The teams intersected as they walked to the benches, the Fannie Lou players looking like bubbles floating in the air bumping into each other, the South Bronx Prep kids walking like the kids whose parents are forcing them to leave early from the park. They were a stove-in team in the wake of Charles's dunk.

I calmly grabbed my clipboard, and we switched defenses to a half-court 2–2–1. We needed a stop, but Rucker was too fast to be corralled by this defense and soared through it. South Bronx Prep scored.

It was 54–51 with thirty seconds left. Frankie found a cutting

Walfri, who was fouled. This was not good. Free-throw shooting had been a constant unsolvable problem all year for him.

They think they fouled the right guy. But I know they fouled the wrong guy. In a move of total redemption, Walfri nailed both free throws to put us up five again. As calculating as a vengeful librarian, he looked at the South Bronx Prep bench with his right finger to his lip, directing a sibilant "Shhh" toward the silent Cougars bench. Just like Rucker did to our bench in January. His eyes said, *Now it's your turn to be silent,* and he trotted back on defense. If Charles's dunk was the highlight of the season, Walfri's cold-blooded gesture was the ribbon it was wrapped in.

After Shamar's two free throws put us up for good, I whispered, "Off the Radar," punching my own hand as though to punctuate the season. Frankie looked up, observed the time and score, and began hopping, skipping, and prancing. He had an astonishing capacity for the big stage.

When the buzzer sounded, the guys ran to hug each other. It allowed the team to celebrate more, and a tidal wave of black jerseys ran off the bench to engulf each other. It was as if a dozen penguins were welcoming one another home. Ty was in tears. My eyes were watering, a dampness I could barely control. I was afraid that if any one of them grabbed me, I would have collapsed in a cascade of tears. If the game in January was *Raging Bull,* this one was *Rocky II.* Instead of yelling "Adrian," I found Nina running down the bleachers into my arms. Jess waved to me with a sleeping Salome in her arms.

Over on the other side of the gym, I saw the Cougars: gone were the displays of arrogance; tears swelled in players' eyes, and one of them looked as if he was mummified on the floor, multiple white towels wrapped around his upper body.

This was the reward for our toil. We didn't yield. We didn't blink. Tensions washed away like street chalk in the rain. The players were eager to share the ball all season, they stretched themselves like elastic on defense, handled the stress of winning, solved the problem of the only team that beat us all season. For a moment winning a city championship transcends any personal pain and etches a historic place in your heart. *Seasons are written in chalk in October. They are not tattooed until March.* I see Michael Castillo, captain of the 2013 team, who always reminds me that he was the most yelled-at player ever. He always said, "Fannie Lou basketball is like a family. My best three friends for life I made on the team." He was sitting next to Ariel Sanchez, one of four 1,000-point scorers in school history, both smiling, enjoying the success of their alma mater. He was right: there was a sense of community in that gym. The former principal Nancy Mann and her husband were there, as were Tony and Steven, the school custodians. People I have worked with for over a decade. We loved the support.

Jessica found me at last. "That was a little stressful. You started winning when Sallie fell asleep. I tried to keep her asleep the rest of the game."

Gaby and I took a selfie with "61–55" sandwiched between our enormous grins.

Each of our last three games, we gave up 55 points. Strange, I thought. Frankie and I hugged and did a one-arm embrace, snapping our fingers.

"Let's do this again next year," I said.

"I got you," he said reassuringly with a triumphant grin.

Coach Paul sat on the chair, immovable. After the last game, all that is with you dies that day. You can't eat. Tears return when no one is looking. You go back to the cold, somber locker room, where only the death rattle of the season can be heard. I've been there. Paul had done a remarkable job building a program from scratch. We were in the same business of trying to turn boys into young men.

A paroxysm of happiness continued at half-court. I was smiling, wiping my eyes, pointing at friends, former players, and coworkers. I have never seen a bunch of kids so happy. They celebrated as if they had landed on the moon. I have never seen a person perform a *gambade* like Cris. It was as if the chemistry in the air had changed. The air was lighter. Cris was floating like the old man in *Mary Poppins* when he starts to sing, "I love to laugh."

I love to win, I thought. Everyone became lighter. I was about to start floating away until I grabbed Salome and Nina. We embraced and they anchored me to the floor. This was not like winning the first title. This feeling was like nothing else I had felt in my life. This is the feeling coaches chase.

HEADWINDS

Winning doesn't soften the blow of poverty. We would like to believe a championship would defeat it. We could drink from the cup of overflowing confidence to become anything we want. But in this life nothing is promised, even as we try to make basketball a sanctuary, however brief. It has allowed me to escape a dysfunctional family and avoid economic determinism, but sometimes a drunk mom will stumble in and change your life.

Living without hope is like gears without a lubricant. We can't live without hope.

After meeting with reporters and friends, a PSAL official grabbed my arm.

"They are going to drench you when you walk in," she warned.

"Huh?" I didn't quite understand.

They wanted to pour water on me because that is what you do when you win. There it was again. Water. I wanted to tell her,

"As everyone knows, meditation and water are wedded forever." But it seems I am always explaining to people how important *Moby-Dick* is to me. In the city we can forget we are on an island. We are surrounded by water. Instead of drowning me in water, we took pictures of the trophy, hugged, laughed. Tears (water) flowed like rivers.

"Team ball beat hero ball tonight!" Tyree said.

"One, two, three, Panthers," we said in unison one last time. "Four, five, six, together."

"Everyone get home safe," I said.

"You too, Coach."

Everyone was embracing; it was deeper than acute intimacy, and it was fulfillment of a shared dream. We took more pictures. I examined the crew after this long journey, with our medals around our necks. I looked heavier, older, and crazier, and they looked thinner, happier, and stronger. And just like that another season ended.

EPILOGUE

Endings are likely to be abrupt, untidy, and, every once in a while, dreamlike, and so it was with the ending of the 2016–17 basketball season. When we returned to school on Monday after the championship game, we received a hero's welcome. The mood in school was upbeat, almost giddy. Everyone, students and staff, wanted to give us their championship game analysis, their favorite play, accompanied by a hug or a smile. Nobody could agree if it was Shamar's pass or Charles's dunk or Walfri's fourth-quarter performance or Ty's floater or Cris's decision making or Frankie's poise that altered the game. It was clear to me it was a culmination of all their plays, augmented by all their resilience *all* season long. We couldn't have dreamed of a better basketball season.

Inevitably, there was talk of next season. We heard comments like "You have a dynasty in the making," or "Next year you guys are going to be even better." I couldn't entertain such thoughts. It seemed inappropriate. People were already preoccupied about the sequel when the movie, in fact, wasn't yet finished. We had to get ready to play La Salle Academy on Friday morning.

Sometimes endings are really not endings. Some guys on the team knew there was something after the city championship. Others had no idea why we had practice after school on Monday. I had to explain, not just to the team and Gaby but to all the staff and students who congratulated us with hugs and smiles, that we still had a chance to win something else: a New York State Federation championship.

After winning the PSAL championship, the winners of each classification—AA (large school), A (medium school), and B (small school)—have a chance to compete in the New York State Federation Tournament of Champions in their respective classifications. The aim of the tournament is to bring together the other three high school organizations—the state public schools (NYSPHSAA), the Catholic schools (CHSAA), and the New York State Association of Independent Schools (NYSAIS)—to crown one state champion.

We drew La Salle, the CHSAA champs, located in the East Village of New York City. If we won, we would play the winner of the other semifinal game, either Westhill, the NYSPHSAA champion from Syracuse, or the Dwight School, the NYSAIS champion from Manhattan. In 2017, the tournament returned to Glens Falls, New York, after a six-year stint in Albany. Glens Falls is about two hundred miles north of New York City. It's a charming town of a little more than fourteen thousand people. Nobody on the team, including me, had ever been this far upstate. Our championship quest had earned us an all-expense-paid weekend trip to the Adirondacks to extend our victory lap.

We had lost some intensity and focus in practice in the days leading up to the Federation game. I think our appetite for winning was sated after beating South Bronx Prep. It was our greatest game of the season and my coaching career. Practicing for another opponent seemed to sully the moment, like disturbing the hypnotized. The team was more excited about the road trip and the hotel than gearing up to play another game.

The tip-off against La Salle was scheduled for 10:45 a.m. Before the game I felt La Salle had a few advantages: size, experience, and depth. During warm-ups I felt those gaps widen. They were intense. The Cardinals looked like a team on their third cup of espresso. When I looked at our warm-ups, it was as if the Panthers needed to hit the snooze button one more time. Once the game started La Salle never looked back. We cut the lead to five at one point in the first half, but La Salle walked away with a 61–47 victory. And for the first time all season, we seemed beguiled. It was like dancing with the lights on way after prom had ended. The loss to La Salle didn't disharmonize the season. The music had stopped a week ago. It was just time to go home. The party was over.

On the bus trip back to the Bronx, I thought about how lucky I was, not in the sense of wins or shooting percentage, but for the devoted team I had and the people who work at and attend Fannie Lou. Jeff Palladino, Fannie Lou's principal, had organized a bus for the 10:45 a.m. game. It was full of early-bird students and staff cheering us on so the dribbles didn't resound alone through the almost empty and frigid Glens Falls Civic Center. (The arena is home to a minor league hockey team.) We had a small cheering section in the arena that warmed my heart. I already knew that we have an incredible school community. I can't overstate the tremendous pleasure it gave the team to see school safety agents, family, custodians, teachers, staff, alumni, and students in the stands. I am unequivocally grateful for their attendance at games, high fives in the hallways, and retweets and likes on social media.

As the bus glided down the New York State Thruway, the team slept. I remember seeing Josh's head resting on JB's shoulder and thinking we had spent so much time together and still they didn't mind the personal proximity. The sun was setting and I was reminded of Hegel, who wrote that "The owl of Minerva [the Roman goddess of wisdom] spreads its wings only at the falling of dusk." That is to say, it's possible to understand what these young men had accomplished only once the season was over. They taught me how to love the game with all its flaws.

I love basketball because it can transport you somewhere,

anywhere, anytime. The Boston Celtics versus the Detroit Pistons in 1987 or the Pinkerton Astros versus the West Blue Devils in 1993 (my last varsity game) or the Fannie Lou Panthers versus the South Bronx Prep Cougars in 2017. Basketball allows you to travel through time. Any game. Any season. Any play. It stays with you.

I now realize how much the team enjoyed the season, how they loved the competition, how they appreciated the small details of a scouting report, how the season helped them get their schoolwork done, and how they never gave up.

At the same time, I wonder how they will adjust now that the season is over. Tyree, Charles, and Kenneth will transition to the volleyball team. Mack will undergo surgery to repair his torn meniscus. Frankie was selected to become an Opportunities Network Fellow, a nonprofit organization that introduces students to the world of finance and business. Bryant, Kaleb, Cris, Josh, and JB tell me they are going to find jobs. Walfri and Shamar will attend Buffalo State in the fall. This was the last few moments we had together. We will never be as close as we were on that bus.

Now that a sense of an ending has settled in, I will finally lose the sense of precariousness I have right before a game. I'm grateful that basketball won't interrupt my thoughts so much. I can also finally recognize that the 2017 Fannie Lou Panthers were dominant all season, especially in the playoffs. We won our first four playoff games by an average of twenty-eight points. However, a championship wasn't inevitable. The championship game easily could have gone in another direction. The effort to find ordinary words for what we accomplished over this extraordinary season is impossible at this moment.

The bus is quiet. There are silent assurances that next season will be successful, but nobody speaks of it. At least not in front of the two seniors, Walfri and Shamar. The returning players have the sense of another phenomenal high school basketball season around the corner. Indeed, the whole team is dreaming about the magic of new beginnings.

Postscript: In the 2017–18 season the Panthers won not just the PSAL championship but the New York State Federation Tournament of Champions, their first state championship.

ACKNOWLEDGMENTS

The process of writing a book about a championship season while at the same time chasing, planning, and dreaming about another championship is what Stefan Zweig in *Chess Story* referred to as "artificial schizophrenia"—this strange process of playing chess against yourself. We won a championship and I finished the book, but at times I wasn't sure if we were winning, losing, or in the middle of a stalemate. What I do know is that I am grateful to those without whose cooperation it would have been impossible.

This book took twelve years to write, if one goes back to my first season coaching; three years in its present form. Over this time, I amassed infinite emotional debt to my wife, Jessica, and our two daughters, Nina and Salome. I amassed, reluctantly, albeit necessarily, piles of drafts, notebooks, books, and articles, which added more clutter to our apartment and hours away from them.

I am eternally grateful for my best buddy, Jack Lafleur, for always talking me off the edge of the cliff after a tough loss or a dispiriting practice. Thanks to my guys, Chris Dietrich, Brent Kendall, and Kevin Scott, for intellectually supporting me during this process.

At Fannie Lou Hamer Freedom High School: thank you to the dedicated staff and to Principal Jeff Palladino.

As the years go by I appreciate Coach Carnovale more and more. I miss him very much.

A special thank-you to Nancy Mann, who read the manuscript and offered meaningful suggestions.

Debts of influence and inspiration and a whole lot of respect to the 2016–17 Fannie Lou Panthers: Gaby Acuria, Kyheem Taylor,

Walfri Restitullo, Shamar Carpenter, Charles Davis, Kenneth Castro, Jaquan Mack, Bryant Gillard, Dalen Ward, Frankie Williams, Tyree Morris, Cris Reyes, Joshua Emanuel, Mohammed Fofana, Alams Beato, Kaleb Stobbs, and Jaelen Bennett.

Thanks to the PSAL and my coaching comrades-in-arms: Paul Campbell, Ben Newman, Chris Ballerini, Lawanda Greene, Matt Calabro, Nigel Thompson, Alain Latortue, Mike King, Anastasia Bitis, and Devon Irving.

I am deeply grateful to the intrepid David McCormick, who never wavered in his support and helped reshape and rethink the manuscript many times over.

This book couldn't have found a more perfect editor and proponent than Gerry Howard. Gerry helped turn the manuscript into *Pounding the Rock*. Thank you to Nora Grubb, his assistant, as well. Unfortunately, I am more talented at drawing plays on a clipboard than typesetting and formatting.

A wicked awesome thank-you to my family: the Skeltons, the Currans, the Kendalls, the Escabis, and the Weinfelds.

Finally, the Bronx has been utterly transformed and renewed in the last thirty years. The efforts of a new generation with steel resilience and brilliant ideas determined to reshape the borough have borne fruit. My greatest debt is to the young men and women who allowed me to teach and coach them. I know they always gave me their best effort. This book is for them.

ABOUT THE AUTHOR

MARC SKELTON is a former all-state basketball guard from Derry, New Hampshire. He graduated from Northeastern University and served two years in the Peace Corps in Moldova, and holds a master's degree in education and political science and received a graduate certificate in Russian studies from Columbia University. He teaches history at Fannie Lou Hamer Freedom High School in the Bronx and has coached the boys' basketball team there since 2006, winning three citywide championships and one state championship.